PIAGET SAMPLER

AN INTRODUCTION TO JEAN PIAGET THROUGH HIS OWN WORDS

Edited by

SARAH F. CAMPBELL, Ph. D.

Kendall College
Evanston, Illinois

JOHN WILEY & SONS, INC.
New York London Sydney Toronto

Library of Congress Cataloging in Publication Data

Piaget, Jean, 1896-
    Piaget's Sampler : An introduction to Jean Piaget through his own words.

    Bibliography: p.
    Includes index.
    1. Cognition (Child psychology) - Addresses, essays, lectures.
I. Title.

BF723.C5P524   155.4'13'08   75-34129

ISBN 0-471-13343-4

ISBN 0-471-13344-2 pbk.

Printed in the United States of America

10 9 8 7 6 5 4 3 2 1

PIAGET
SAMPLER

Wayne Behling/Ypsilanti Press

EDITOR'S PREFACE

This book is the fulfillment of a promise I made some time ago to a class of students to whom I introduced Piaget through his own writings. Their last question to me was, "Why must he be so difficult to read?" With my final wave and farewell, I said, "I'll try to put some of his writings together so that the next class won't find him so hard."

I could have responded, of course, that there are many secondary sources that describe what Piaget is saying, but all of these splendid books contain their own authors' personal understanding and interpretation of Piagetian notions. There still seems to me to be intrinsic value to reading the original words, even though translated.

But the truth exists that Piaget is hard to read: his vocabulary is unique—more and more of which is creeping into our psychological and educational literature; his analytic style teases out implications faster, slower, or more elaborately, than we want; the many repetitions seem like variations on a theme in spite of the fact that he adds new insight with each repetition; the sentences are ponderously long; and readers are overwhelmed with his breadth of knowledge in many different fields.

The most compelling force for me to compile this book was in one sense to repay the truly wonderful experience I had with that particular class—summer graduate students, most of whom were teachers. Near the beginning of the course they reflected many of the stereotypes that adults have of children's behavior: children play and tease and baffle, ask a lot of questions without understanding our answers; children challenge their adults; they're selfish and unthinking; they want to touch and manipulate things when it's time to do serious "work."

I asked the students to read several of Piaget's books as groups and to report to the class on what they could understand from the reading. They found it hard going, even with support from their peers, but very capable reports resulted. Since the students tested some of the notions experimentally when they doubted what he said, the reports included taped interviews, pictures drawn by children, and sample protocols.[1] Almost all of the students volunteered that, as the result of having read some Piaget and having shared their understandings with others, they now understood children! Now they could see that the aspects of children that they complained about are just the characteristics that are essential in the development of children's intelligence. Somehow the business in which teachers are engaged bears a connection with the development of children's intelligence!

I originally intended to put together excerpts, not snippets, from the things Piaget has written, deleting repetitions, cutting sentences here and there, finding some of the pieces that are not as well known and gathering them into a sampler. Someone else might have sampled differently. I had one direction from Professor Piaget himself: do not duplicate the book by Molly Brearley and Elizabeth Hitchfield.[2] Theirs is a delightful little book, describing some of the experiments that are classics, but much of it is not in Piaget's own words, whereas my intention is to keep his words.

I tried to sample over the time span of his writing, over the subject matter, and over the degrees to which his works are familiar to readers of English. Some of the selections have not appeared in English before and have been translated by me and my colleague, Dr. Elizabeth Rüt-schi-Herrmann.

But, instead of thinking of a sampler as a sifter, there is another analogy that is more appropriate in the Piagetian sense. Many generations back, little girls used to construct a sampler. It was a picture in needlework that was an exercise in sewing, letters, numbers, spatial relations, borders, blending of colors, creating pictures, and whatever else took the little girl's fancy when she was provided with a piece of coarse canvas, a needle, a thimble, and a hank of colored threads. Often the child made more than one alphabet, each progression showing more elaborate lettering, more elaborate stitchery, and more variety in

---

[1]"Protocol" is the record of the sequential verbal exchange between interrogator and child, including a description of gestures, where they were recorded.

[2]Molly Brearley, and Elizabeth Hitchfield, *A Guide to Reading Piaget*. New York: Schocken Books, 1966. This book contains descriptions of several Piagetian tasks.

coloration. Sometimes she was able to stay within the borders that she constructed for herself, sometimes not; sometimes the pattern she started was completed, sometimes not. Some samplers (maybe those that were tucked away and saved) were just stages toward another sampler that would be singled out for display and recognition by family and friends. A successful sampler was part of the rites of passage from childhood to womanhood. Thus, this book, as a sampler, is intended for the reader's own construction of the theory of Piaget.

In order to construct Piaget's notions, there are a few traditional modes from which we must try to disentangle ourselves. One is the notion that norms exist. Maybe they do, because some have been found, but try to forget this, and let Piaget show the point of view that each child literally makes up his own mind (his intelligence) by the actions that he performs on objects, in his own time. Another tendency is to assume that intelligence is something that exists, gets measured, and that the measure is forever the individual's mark somehow connected with his rank in society. To understand Piaget, try to assume, instead, that each person has intelligence. That shouldn't be too hard. In this volume you will see that intelligence grows within the person, that this capacity is changing, evolving, growing stage upon stage, so that adult thinking is not the same as childish thinking, but it grows out of childish thinking. Then, there is the American tendency to push or prod so that stages follow faster one upon another. If we can forget the competitiveness inherent in this assumption and substitute the assumption of cooperation, Piaget tells us that this intelligence we prize for our children grows out of cooperative exchange between the child and his environment, which includes us adults. I am not trying to interpret Piaget but, instead, am urging the reader to substitute for notions of norm, IQ, and competition equally valid notions of individuality, universal intelligence, and cooperation.

Where do you start to read this book? Is the order in which the samples appear of particular importance? No. Read what you can and assimilate the words. They may sound strange. As you find them in different contexts, they will begin to have meaning. The reader brings to the printed page certain preconcepts about what Piaget is all about. Maybe you have read about him in a secondary source. There is no secondary source that tells all about Piaget; he has written too much, said too much, and has had too much said about him for you to understand him completely. If your reading this volume takes you to other writings of Piaget, so much the better; you have some reading cut out for yourself!

One can hardly be Piagetian and say that order is not important. But the chronological order of writing or translation does not fit the developmental order within the child, as Piaget sees it. People are apt to speak of Early, Middle, and Recent Piaget, and for each period of his work there is a special meaning for his theory, but I suggest that you read the "Autobiography" (Chapter 10). If you want to see order, maybe this chapter is the place to start. I included it at the end because it is the longest selection and I recognize that everyone does not ask the question *Who is the person?* first, although it probably will arise at some point. The "Autobiography" tells much more than who Piaget is; maybe you can glean some of the important points of his work and the relationships among the research from reading it. It will be of particular interest to those who already have considerable knowledge of Piaget, because the last part of the chapter was translated specifically for this book and it may be unfamiliar.

Other questions that will be asked are *What does he say?* and *How does he know?* I'm not interpreting Piaget when I answer the second question: he knows by his *méthode clinique,* by asking children questions and more questions. There are two selections that partly explain how he used this method. The one on the developmental use of "because" in the reasoning of the child (Chapter 3) has been taken from one of his early studies and illustrates how he asked questions of the children and what he did with their answers. Notice how he avoids statistics in the American sense. The original version was more than twice as long (and contained more points). Lengthy reports are typical of Early Piaget. His more recent writings do not include the teasing analyses, the testing, nor the repetitions, and therefore they are easier for us to read. Another selection (sometimes referred to but not located in the usual sources) is the one called "Transition from Egocentricity to Reciprocity" (Chapter 4). It discusses the child's developing notions of the homeland, and it includes another illustration of the use of Piaget's method. He investigated this area of thinking early and included it in the same *Judgment and Reasoning of the Child* volume that he originally wrote in 1924. However, the piece contained here as Chapter 4 is much more recent (1951).

During Piaget's Middle period he investigated the roots of that intelligence, which he found in children who could talk to him, by studying his own three children. I did not include any of those studies because Chapter 8, "Behaviour of Babies" in Brearley and Hitchfield[3] already describes some of the results. The period studied, the sensori-motor period, is also described briefly by Piaget in "Development Explains Learning" (Chapter 6) and, more completely, in "Stages and Their

[3] *Ibid.*

Properties in the Development of Thinking" (Chapter 1). He has more
to say about it in Chapter 10, "Autobiography." So, although this aspect of intelligence comes first in the development of children, it was
not the first to be investigated.

Perhaps a corollary to the question *How does he know?* is *How do I
know?* How do *you* know that what children say in response to the
kinds of inquiries into children's thinking that Piaget makes is accurate or holds true for the kind of children you know? The most obvious
answer is *Try it!.* My students did that and, in amazement, found that
what was reported is substantially true. You will find many of the tasks
and questions he has used reported, most of them using very simple
equipment like jars of different shapes and two balls of clay, depending
of course on the ages of the children you will be querying.

As for the question *What does Piaget say?,* there is a wealth of his
own writings. In this volume I included what to me is one of his most
straightforward statements about some of the things he says, the piece
called "Stages and Their Properties in the Development of Thinking"
(Chapter 1). Another shorter piece is a summary statement from his
recent book *Insights and Illusions of Philosophy,* which has nothing to
do with philosophy in the piece I have excerpted, called "What Intelligence Is" (Chapter 2). This statement is a little more abstract than the
longer one. A good selection to read after either or both of these is "The
Adolescent as a Total Personality" (Chapter 5), because it describes
adolescent and adult thinking more concretely than the summary
statement, and it gives further extensions of what the implications are.
It is from the book whose senior author is Piaget's associate, Bärbel
Inhelder. Although the experimental work reported is by Mlle. Inhelder, the portion from which this piece was taken was written jointly
with Professor Piaget (according to the preface of that book).

If you are the kind of person who likes a nice model to follow, a
diagram to put on the board, or a map to look at, you may enjoy the
piece called "A Feedback Model of Cognitive Functioning" (Chapter 9).
This came rather recently and it is not frequently mentioned, but it
paves the way for a rather elaborate model of equilibration which he
has developed very recently and which is much too complicated to be
included here. This chapter may make difficult reading. This particular
piece (Chapter 9) came from a book in which Piaget wrote only the
introduction, because it dealt with the work on memory conducted by
his associates and students in Geneva, an area in which he was not too
concerned at the time. But he developed the discussion and theory as
an introduction to the collection of experiments. The problem of memory is an example of serendipidy in the Piaget group. Read the piece

called "How the Problem of Memory Came About" (Chapter 7), and see how his great mind was able to develop among his collaborators some interesting ideas.

As you read, if you have a background in American or British psychology, you may wonder where his theorizing fits in and whether he ignores all of the stimulus-response psychology. Not so. To illustrate how well Piaget attends to what is going on in psychology outside of Switzerland, Chapter 6 includes an answer to what Piaget refers to as the "American question" (can the stages be hurried by special instruction), and is presented here as a kind of tag to some other interesting points about factors that influence mental development. It is just part of a lecture given to an American audience, the entire text of which is not available in bookstores.

The connection between cognitive development and the affective is shown in Piaget's remarkable application of his theory in the article "Will and Action" (Chapter 8) to a problem posed long ago by William James. This too is a reference seldom found and quoted, but seems to be an example of the highest kind of thinking, and it truly adds to our conception of some of the depths in fields other than his own of which Piaget is capable.

This book is intended for anyone who comes into contact with children, teachers, parents, and parents-to-be, and I sincerely hope that understanding Piaget will enrich the understanding and appreciation of children.

Sarah F. Campbell

NOTE
TO THE STUDENT

Some of the books by Jean Piaget used in this volume may be procured in paperback editions:

Insights and Illusions of Philosophy (Translated by Wolfe Mays). New York: The World Publishing Company (Meridian Books M235), 1971.

Judgment and Reasoning in the Child (Translated by Marjorie Warden). Paterson, New Jersey: Littlefield, Adams & Co. (N., 205), 1964.

Piaget Rediscovered: A Report of the Conference on Cognitive Studies and Curriculum Development, March 1964, Richard E. Ripple and Verne N. Rockcastle (editors). Ithaca: Cornell University School of Education. (Send $2.50 payable to Cornell University, and order from The Mailing Room, Building 7, Research Park, Cornell University, Ithaca, New York, 14850.)

The Growth of Logical Thinking from Childhood to Adolescence (by Bärbel Inhelder and Jean Piaget) (Translated by Anne Parsons and Stanley Milgram). New York: Basic Books, Inc., 1958.

S. F. C.

CONTENTS

1

STAGES AND THEIR PROPERTIES
IN THE DEVELOPMENT OF THINKING

The Attainment of Invariants and Reversible Operations in the Development of Thinking

It is the aim of the present essay to introduce American readers to our more recent studies of children's thinking and the development of intelligence. Only my very early books have been available for many years in English translation. The investigations that we have conducted since then are largely unknown on this side of the Atlantic ocean. In the presentation to follow I would like to sketch this work briefly, and to illustrate it with concrete examples from our experiments.

An important difference between our older studies and our present ones pertains to their method: Initially we relied exclusively on interviews and asked the children only verbal questions. This may have been a beginning, and it can yield certain types of results but, assuredly, it is not exhaustive. Of late, our investigations have been conducted quite differently. We now try to start with some action that the child must perform. We introduce him into an experimental setting, present him with objects and—after the problem has been stated—the child must do something, he must experiment. Having observed his actions and manipulation of objects we can then pose the verbal questions that constitute the interview. Note that this interview now

From *Social Research*, 1963, *30*: 283–299. Copyright © *Social Research*, Autumn, 1963. Reprinted with permission.

pertains to a preceding action, and this seems to me to be a more fruitful and reliable method than the purely verbal inquiry.

Furthermore, while our earlier studies pertained to various classes of thought content, we later became increasingly more interested in the formal aspects of thought. The aspects transcend any single content category and provide the basis for the intellectual elaboration of any and all contents. During the past few years our essential preoccupation has been the analysis of those complex structures[1] of thought that seem to characterize the various developmental stages. Complex structures at the highest level are those systems of operations[2]—be they themselves relatively simple or complex—that make the total operation possible. I shall emphasize primarily one aspect of these structures, namely their reversibility. I use the term reversibility in its logical or mathematical sense, not in its physiological or medical connotation. I believe intelligence is above all characterized by the coordination of operations that are reversible actions.

Basically, to solve a problem is to coordinate operations while focusing on the solution. An operation is, first of all, an action. We shall see that at its inception intelligence begins with simple actions on the sensori-motor level, actions which then become interiorized and come to be represented symbolically. Moreover, operations are basically actions which can be performed in either direction, that is, actions which are reversible. This is really the remarkable thing about intelligence, if one compares intelligence with other mental functions, for instance habits. Habits are not reversible, they are oriented in one direction only. Thus, we have learned to write from left to right, and if we wanted to write from right to left we could not do so on the basis of our previous habits, we would have to start learning a new habit. By contrast, once we can handle an operation, for instance the operation of adding in the arithmetical sense, or in its more general logical sense, we can reverse that specific action. From the moment when the child understands what it means to add, that is, to bring together two groups to form one, he implicitly knows also what it means to separate the groups again, to dissociate them, to subtract. It is of the same operation; he can work it one way, in one direction, and also the other way, in the opposite direction. This reversibility is not a primitive matter; it is progressively built up as a function of the same complex structures mentioned above. From the psychological point of view, one of the most fruitful terrains for the analysis of this reversibility is the problem of conservation.

[1] *Editor's note.* Piaget defines structure as "... a form of organization of experience." Battro, Antonio, *Piaget: Dictionary of Terms,* translated and edited by Elizabeth Rütschi-Herrmann, and Sarah F. Campbell, New York: Pergamon Press, 1973. p. 168.

[2] Definition: "... interiorized actions or interiorizable actions, reversible and coordinated in total structures." Battro, p. 121.

In any system of reversible actions there results the construction of certain invariants, certain forms of conservation analogue to those subserving scientific reasoning. In the young child we can observe the development of these invariants, and the evolution of concepts of conservation. For instance, we can ask a child whether, when a given liquid is being poured from a container A into another container B of a different shape, the quantity of the liquid remains the same. For us that is self-evident, as it is for children above a certain age. But we shall see that for the younger children it is not self-evident at all. In fact, they will say that the quantity has increased because the height of the new container is greater, or that it is less because container B is thinner. They have not yet attained the logically relevant concept of conservation and the pertinent invariants, and they cannot grasp these until some time later when their thinking becomes capable of reversible operations, and when these operations become coordinated structures. The immediate result of the achievement of such structures is not only the affirmation of certain forms of conservation, but, at the same time, the insight that this conservation is self-evident, logically necessary, precisely because it arises from the coordination of operations. Let us trace now, step by step, the development of this reversibility, of these forms of conservation and also of certain complex structures.

I shall distinguish four stages in this development: (1) the pre-language sensori-motor stage; (2) the pre-operational stage from 2–7 years; (3) the stage of concrete operations between the approximate ages of 7 and 12; (4) finally the stage of propositional operations with their formal characteristics which are attained at the pre-adolescent and adolescent stage.

THE PRE-LANGUAGE STAGE

We need to say only a few words about the sensori-motor stage. This period is important because during it are developed substructures essential for later operations. At the present time everybody agrees that there is intelligent action prior to language. The baby demonstrates intelligent behavior before he can speak. Interestingly, we note, the earliest forms of intelligence already aim at the construction of certain invariants—practical invariants to be sure, namely invariants of the concrete space of immediate action. These first invariants are already the result of a sort of reversibility but it is a practical reversibility embedded in the very actions; it is not yet a constituent of thought proper. Of the invariants which arise at the sensori-motor stage perhaps the most important one is the schema of the permanent object. I call the permanent object that object which continues to exist outside of the perceptual field. A perceived object is not permanent object in that sense. I would say that there is no schema of a permanent object if the child no longer reacts once the object has disappeared from the perceptual field, when it is no longer visible, when it can no longer be touched, when it is no longer heard. On the other hand I would say that there is already an invariant, a schema of the permanent object, if the child begins to search for the vanished object. Such a schema is not present from the very beginning. When, at about 4½ months of age, a child starts to reach for the things he sees in his visual field and, when he begins to coordinate vision and prehension to some extent, one can observe that he does not yet react to a permanent object. For instance, I may show the infant a watch, dangling it in front of him. He reaches out to take the watch, but at the very moment when he has already extended his hand, I cover the watch with a napkin. What happens? He promptly withdraws his hand as if the watch had been absorbed into the napkin. Even though he can very well remove the napkin if it is put over his own face, he does not lift it in order to look for the watch underneath. You might say that the watch is perhaps of no great interest to the infant: however, the same experiment can be made with a nursing bottle. I have done this with one of my children at the age of 7 months. At the time of his feeding I show him the bottle, he extends his hand to take it, but, at that moment, I hide it behind my arm. If he sees one end sticking out he kicks and screams and gives every indication of wanting to have it. If, however, the bottle is completely hidden and nothing sticks out, he stops crying and acts for all we know as if the bottle no longer existed, as if it had been dissolved and absorbed into my arm.

Towards the end of the first year the infant begins to search for the vanished object. Already at 9 to 10 months he looks for it behind a screen. If we place the child between two screens, for example, a cloth or a pillow on his right and another one at his left, we can make a very curious observation concerning the locus of the hiding place. With the child in that position I now show him, for instance, a watch. As soon as he evinces interest in the watch I place it under the cloth to his right. Thereupon the child will promptly lift the cloth and grasp the watch. Now I take it from him and, very slowly, so that he can follow with his eyes, move the watch over to his left side. Then, having made sure that he has indeed followed the movement, I cover the watch in its new position. I have observed this in my three children over varying periods of time, and we have repeated this experiment frequently since. There is a stage when, at the moment the child sees the watch disappear at the left, he immediately turns back to the right and looks for the watch there. In other words, he looks for the object where he has found it before. The object is not yet a mobile thing, capable of movements and correlated displacements in an autonomous system in space. Rather, the object is still an extension of the action itself, an action that is repeated where and how it was successful the first time around.

Finally, towards the end of the first year the object comes to have a degree of independent existence. Its disappearance elicits search, and that search is guided by the observed displacements. Now we can speak of a structure of coordinated displacements or, indeed, a group of displacements in the sense in which the term is used in geometry with the implication of the possibilities of movement in one direction and in reverse as well as of detours by means of which the same goal can be reached over a variety of alternate pathways. A long time ago Henri Poincaré advanced the hypothesis that primitive sensori-motor space must originate from such groups of displacements.[3] Without entering into the details of that discussion, I should like to point out that this group structure—which is already a reversible structure—is not an *a priori* given, as Poincaré would have us believe. Instead, it develops gradually during the first year. The attainment of the notion of the permanent object is the exact correlate of the emerging organization of reversible movements that constitute the groups of displacements. You could say that the permanent object is the first group invariant, provided it is understood that a group at this level is not yet a system of operations but merely a system of practical actions in the immediate space. This system enables the individual to take account of successive displacements, to order them, then reverse them, and so forth.

THE PRE-OPERATIONAL STAGE

Let us turn now to the development of representational thinking proper. We observe it first in play, in imaginary games with their fictitious qualities and symbolic aspects, play in which one thing comes to be represented by means of another thing. Differentiated imitation, for instance of various people in the child's environment, and a variety of other symbolic acts belong to this stage. Such representational thinking greatly enlarges the range of intellectual activity. The latter no longer pertains only to the nearby space, the present moment and the action in progress. Thanks to representational thought such activity can now be applied with reference to far away space, to events outside the immediate perceptual sphere, to the past which can be recovered and recounted, and to the future in the form of plans and projects. In

[3]Henri Poincaré, "The Value of Science," in *The Foundations of Science* (Lancaster, Pa.: The Science Press, 1940), Chaps. III and IV.

other words the universe of representation is obviously much wider
than the universe of direct action. Consequently, the first tools that
have already been developed at the sensori-motor level cannot be applied immediately to this wider sphere, they cannot be generalized
immediately in their broader relevance. The child must now recon-
struct on an ideational plane the invariants, the forms of coordination
whose beginnings we observed at the sensori-motor level. All this takes
place in the period which extends from the beginning of language at
one end to the age of about seven or eight years at the other end. During
this period we can already speak of thought, of representation, but not
yet of logical operations defined as interiorized reversible action systems. In children within this age range we have studied all sorts of
problems of conservation and invariants, and we have found quite
systematically that these notions of conservation begin to develop only
at about the age of seven or eight years.

I shall not come back to the problem of liquids being poured from one
container into another, but we can make the same experiment with
beads. We can ask the child to put blue beads into container A and red
beads into container B, and we make sure that each time he places a
blue bead into container A he also places a red bead into the other
container B, so that there will be the same number of beads in each of
the two containers. The child is then told to pour the beads from
container B into a new container C, thereupon we ask him if there are
the same number of beads in C as in A—those in A having remained
there and those from B having been poured into C. Now a curious thing
happens. Until approximately the age of 6½ years the child believes
that the number of beads has changed, that there are more beads in
container C because it is higher than B, or that there are fewer beads
in container C because it is thinner than B. If you ask him "Where do
these extra beads come from?" or "What happened to the beads that
are no longer there?" he is very much surprised at your question. He
is totally uninterested in the mechanism of the transformation. What
interests him is the gross perceptual configuration which is different
in the two situations; even in the case of these discrete entities there
is no conservation of absolute quantities.

The same can be shown with respect to the correspondence of numbers. You can make the following experiment. The child is presented
with an alignment of six blue poker chips, one next to the other, and
is given a box of red poker chips with the request to construct a similar
array with as many red poker chips as there are blue poker chips in
the model. Here we find three stages, two of them belonging to the
period now under discussion. There is a primitive stage at approximately 4 to 4½ years when the child simply places chips in a line of

similar length without regard for any one-to-one correspondence of the components. Thus, he defines quantity essentially in terms of occupied space.

The second stage is much more interesting and lasts approximately to age 6½ to 7 years. Here we find exact correspondence between the number of the chips in the model and those placed by the child. Many authors have been satisfied with this visual correspondence, and they have concluded that it is proof of the child's understanding of numbers. We can show, however, that this is not the case. All you have to do is to spread the chips of one of the two groups a little further apart, or to push them closer together, and the child will no longer think that the two alignments contain identical quantities. As soon as visual correspondence is destroyed, the one-to-one correspondence of numbers-of-action is abolished. In other words, the equivalence that the child had produced was only one of the perceptual configuration, a construction which is not yet an operation in our sense. As the configuration changes, the equivalence disappears, and there is no conservation of quantity.

We can study the problem of conservation of quantity also in the realm of space. For example, we draw two parallel lines of the same length whose endpoints lie directly underneath one another; then we shift one of the lines to the right or the left. Under these conditions some children tell us that one line is longer because it extends beyond the other one at the left, or that the first is shorter because the second projects beyond the first one on the right. I have seen some children who, at approximately age seven, suddenly discovered the conservation of length during this experiment. First they said that one line is longer, then that the other line is longer, and then all at once, they said: "No, they are the same. You have moved this line, and that makes a difference at one end, but there is the same difference at the other, and so it is really the same all along." This may seem to you very complicated reasoning to arrive at a notion which is obvious to us, but it is not at all obvious at a level when the invariant relationships between beginning and end are not yet firmly established with respect to length.

The same is true for conservation of distance. We have shown the child a model of two trees, asking him to tell us whether they were close together or far apart in order to establish these concepts. Then we put a wall between the two trees, a box for instance, and I expected that the children would tell us now that the trees were further apart than before, because there is a barrier between them. I reasoned in motor terms, but the children did not. Fortunately psychology is an experimental science and we often find the opposite of what we expect. In this situation children between five and six and a half have explained to me that the distance is less now than before because the linear distance occupied by the barrier does not count. Near and far refer to empty space between objects; the space occupied by the box is not empty and therefore it does not count. One child said to me: "Of course if you had a hole in the wall, it would be the same as before." So we constructed a wall with a hole and a shutter, so that we could open and close the hole. Now indeed we observed that the distance remained unchanged in the eyes of the children as long as the hole remained open, even though they continued to assert that the distance was less as soon as the aperture was closed. These experiments are interesting because they demonstrate not only the impact of the perceptual configuration, which we have mentioned before, but even as influenced by certain perceptual illusions—for example, contrast effects. Perceptually speaking, a straight line and an empty space do not have identical spatial values, and their perceptual difference manifests itself here at the representational level.

Another example is the following: We confront the child with two identical green cardboards and tell him that these are two pastures where cows can graze. Both have lots of grass, so much, in fact, that if you put a cow half-way between the two she cannot decide which one to choose. At this point the child readily agrees that obviously the two pastures must be equal. Now the farmer who owns the first pasture puts up a house in one corner. The second farmer, who owns the other pasture, builds exactly the same kind of house but, instead of putting it in the corner he puts it right in the middle of the pasture. Do equal amounts of grass remain in the two pastures now? Already here the configuration is somewhat different but you see a good number of children who will tell you that it is the same on both pastures when there is only one house. Next, the first farmer puts up another house adjoining the first one in the corner, and the second farmer puts another one here, adjoining the one in the middle. Are there still equal amounts of grass to be had from the two pastures? Starting with two houses it has become complicated. There are children who will tell us that there is lots more grass in the one pasture than in the other. Remember Euclid's theorem that if you take two equal quantities from two equal quantities there remain two equal quantities? That is the same logic that presupposes conservation, but here we have no conservation and Euclid's axiom is not yet valid for the 5-year-old.

THE STAGE OF CONCRETE OPERATIONS

Towards the age of seven or so the problems of conservation become resolved. There are a few exceptions that concern complex quantities, for instance weight or volume, but simple quantities such as collections or lengths are no longer problematical. How have they been resolved? They have been resolved as a function of three arguments which children always give you, irrespective of the experimental problem. The first argument is: the quantity, or the number is the same—for example, in the bead problem, nothing has been added and nothing has been taken away. I call this the identity argument, because it takes place entirely within the single, self-contained system without any attempt at transcending the boundaries of that system. This argument is certainly not the true root of the attainment of conservation, because the younger children also know very well that nothing has been added or taken away. The real problem is to know why this becomes an argument for the child at a given moment, when it was not an argument for him before.

The child's second argument tells us the reason. I call this the argument of simple reversibility. The child says: "You have done nothing except to pour the beads in the other container, so it looks different, but all you have to do is to pour them back and you will see that they are the same." In other words, it is no longer the perceptual configuration which is interesting, it is their displacement and the resultant transformation. This transformation is apprehended as something that can take place in both directions, that is reversible. Now we understand the first argument concerning the identity of the beads. Identity is precisely the product of the original operation and its reversal; it has attained the status of a system as a function of this simple reversibility.

The third argument used by the children is again based on a kind of reversibility, but now in the form of a pattern of relationships. The child tells you: "Here is more height but a little less width; what you gain in height you lose in width; that evens it out." This implies a pattern of relationships, a multiplication of relationships and their mutual compensation; it is once more a type of reversibility. In other words these three arguments, that of identity, that of simple reversibility and that of patterned relationships show you the beginnings of operations as we have defined them. These operations, that can be observed between the ages of seven years and eleven or twelve years, are already logical operations. Their structure is essentially logical, even though the available implications of that logic are still rather limited. They are only operations of classes and relations and are not yet operations of the logic of propositions. They do not even contain all the operations possible with classes and relations, but only certain rather elementary systems that can be understood by the child as they relate to concrete *manipulanda*. These operations always center around an action or an application to specific objects. For this reason we call them "concrete operations." We use the term "operational groupings" to designate those elementary and immediate systems of action which are patterned as they occur in spatial and temporal contiguity; these simple systems do not yet include all of the logic of classes and relations.

Here is another example of such an operational grouping. The problem is one of inclusion, that is, the inclusion of a class A in a class B with the complement of A', of inclusion of class B in a class C with the complement of B' etc. In this case you have a very simple system in which the addition of two classes results in a new class from which substraction of one leads back to the first class, a tautology with rather limited possibilities. This structure first appears at about age seven and, it seems to me, is basic for the notion of conservation. It is impossible to conduct such operations without invariants and without conservation, precisely because the necessary invariant of these operations is the conservation of the total system. We can experimentally show that this is the case by testing the relationship of inclusion of A in B. You present the child with an open box that contains wooden beads. The child knows they are all wooden because he handles them, touching each and finding that it is made of wood. Most of these beads are brown, but a few are white. The problem we pose is simply this: are there more brown beads or more wooden beads? Let us call A the brown beads, B the wooden beads: then the problem is simply that of the inclusion of A in B. This is a very difficult problem before the age of 7 years. The child states that all the beads are wooden, states that most of them are brown and a few are white, but if you ask him if there are more brown beads or more wooden beads he immediately answers: "There are more brown ones because there are only two or three white ones." So you say: "Listen, this is not what I am asking. I don't want to know whether there are more brown or more white beads, I want to know whether there are more brown beads or more wooden beads." And, in order to make it easier, I take an empty box and place it next to the one with the beads and I ask: "If I were to put the wooden beads into that box would any remain in this one?" The child answers: "No, none would be left because they are all wooden." Then I say: "If I were to take the brown beads and put them into that box, would any be left in this one?" The child replies: "Of course, two or three white ones would remain." Apparently he has now understood the situation, the fact that all the beads are wooden and that some are not brown. So I ask him once more: "Are there more brown beads or more wooden beads?" Now it is evident that the child begins to understand the problem, see that there is indeed a problem, that matters are not as simple as they seemed at first. As we watch him we observe that he is thinking very hard. Finally he concludes: "But there are still more brown beads; if you take the brown ones away, only two or three white beads remain."

Why does this answer recur? Because the child can reason about the whole as long as it is not broken up into parts or, if we force him to break it up, he can reason about the parts, but he cannot reason simultaneously about the whole and the parts. If he is pushed to deal with the brown beads, then the whole no longer exists, it is divided into the two components, the brown beads and the white beads. In order to reunite one part with the whole, the child must not only be capable of the reasoning involved, he must at the same time understand that one part is always the whole minus the other part, and that presupposes conservation of the whole, conservation which results here from simple grouping operations involving classes. This system is psychologically so interesting because it is one of the basic systems which mediate the notions of conservation.

THE STAGE OF PROPOSITIONAL OPERATIONS[4]

Let us proceed to the last stage which begins approximately at the age of 12 years and which is characteristic of the whole adolescent development. This is the period during which new logical operations appear: propositional operations, the logic of propositions, implication, and so forth. These are superimposed onto the earlier concrete operations. The adolescent is no longer limited to concrete reasoning about objects, he begins to reason hypothetically. Starting from a theoretical assumption he can reason that if it is true, then certain consequences must follow. This is the hypothetico deductive method that presupposes implication, disjunction, compatibility, and all the other operations of the logic of propositions. The psychological problem here is first of all to discover how the logic of propositions develops, how it arises out of the concrete operations discussed above. Moreover, at the same stage —that is, starting at about the age of 12 years, there appear not only propositional operations but also, and very striking, a host of other types of new operations which, at first glance, have no relationship to the propositional operations.

There are for instance what the mathematicians call combinatorial operations. Let me illustrate these by the results of another experiment. We present the child with piles of red, blue, green, and yellow poker chips and set him the task to make all possible combinations of pairs, or all possible combinations of three or four colors. At the level

---

[4] *Editor's note.* Often called formal operations.

of concrete operations, up to age twelve or so, the child can produce a number of such groups and combinations, and can do so correctly, but he is unable to find a systematic method by means of which he can arrive at all possible combinations. By contrast, around age twelve the child begins to find a practical method that will permit him to make all possible combinations, even though he has not had any instruction concerning combinatorial operations nor learned the proper mathematical formula.

More or less simultaneously we observe at the same stage the appearance of operations which involve proportions. This too we can study experimentally, for instance by means of balance problems where weights and distances can be varied. Here the child discovers that a given weight A at distance B from the fulcrum is equal to weight B at distance A, and he thus comes to establish proportions between weights and distances. Also at approximately the same time operations involving probabilities first appear, operations which involve the consideration of probable and possible events. Finally, certain additional types of operations also enter during this stage, operations which we shall leave aside in the present discussion.

Two fundamental psychological questions arise in connection with this last stage. The first concerns the nature and development of the logic of propositions. Secondly, we must ask why the logic of propositions appears at the same time as such other systems of operation as combinations, proportions, and so forth, that have at first sight no particular relationship either among each other or to the logic of propositions. Here the concept of complex structures appears to me to be especially valuable. Let us take, for instance, the well-known sixteen basic operations of the logic of propositions. If you compare their structure to the structure of concrete operations, you see immediately that there are marked differences. The former is a lattice-type structure in the usual mathematical meaning of that term, a complete lattice, while the latter has an incomplete lattice structure, with a join for any two positions, but lacking meets for classes of the same rank.[5] It is a semi-lattice, and so are all the groups of concrete operations: they may have joins and lack meets, or they may contain meets but lack joins. As soon as you deal with propositional logic, however, you have the basic four-

[5]In the introduction of Piaget's *Logic and Psychology* (New York: Basic Books, 1957), W. Mays gives the following definitions (p. xv): "Boolean algebra may be considered as a special case of certain abstract mathematical systems called lattices. A lattice has certain limiting conditions—*join* and *meet*. In the case of any two classes X and Y, the *join* is the smallest of the classes in which X and Y are both included, and the *meet* is the largest class included both in X and Y." (Italics in original.)

fold table[6] which, to be sure, looks as if it might represent simply the multiplication of classes, that is, which apparently resembles one of the systems already available at a more concrete level.

The great new achievement at this level is the fact that the sixteen binary operations of two-valued propositional logic are systematically derived from the four basic conjunctions. In other words, the attainment of propositional logic presupposes a lattice structure which has evolved from the semi-lattice structures implied by the operations at the earlier, more concrete level, and which is the direct result of the generalization of classification. The lattice is the schema of all possible classifications which can be derived from its elements but, at the same time, the lattice has combinatorial characteristics. From the psychological point of view it is very striking to find the simultaneous appearance of propositional operations on the one hand, operations which presuppose a lattice structure and thus combinatorial operations and, on the other hand, combinatorial operations applied to mathematical problems. The child is of course not aware of the identity of the structure of these apparently different operations, an identity which our analysis has convincingly demonstrated.

Now as to proportions—how are we to explain the appearance of proportions at the same stage? Let us remember that propositional operations do not only constitute a lattice, they also constitute a group. If you take any operation, such as implication, you can reverse it—that is, state its negative, and you can determine its reciprocal, as well as the negative of the reciprocal. The latter I would like to call its correlative. Here we have a group of four transformations, logical transformations to be sure, but transformations from which you can nevertheless derive a system of proportions. This system results from the application of simple operations to a single proposition.

Perhaps this seems a very abstract explanation. Let us go back, therefore, to concrete observations, and let us find out how the child comes to discover proportions. He discovers proportions through experience, for instance as he finds out that adding weight on a balance produces the same result as increasing a constant weight's distance from the fulcrum, and vice versa, that he can lighten the load by decreasing either weight or distance. In this way he learns the equivalence of two transformations. At the same time he discovers reciprocals

[6]Note 2, pp. xi–xiv and p. 34. For detail the reader may consult any good introductory text, for example, S. K. Langer, *An Introduction to Symbolic Logic,* second revised edition (New York: Dover, 1953). The interested reader is referred also to the treatment by the author of Alice in Wonderland, Lewis Carroll, in his *Symbolic Logic, Part I Elementary* (London: Macmillan, 1897).

—that is, if he increases the weight he must decrease the distance, if he increases the distance he must decrease the weight in order to maintain equilibrium. The child does of course not know these special terms, he expresses himself in simple, everyday language, but his language describes his reasoning exactly. He states that increasing the weight while decreasing the distance gives the same result as decreasing the weight and increasing the distance, and this is a statement of proportions.

CONCLUSION

I suggest that the structure of propositional operations is a complex structure which comprises both lattices and groups. Such a structure has many possibilities and implications. These may remain potentialities only, or they may be realized when there arises a problem requiring propositional operations. Let me add that this hypothesis is not only of psychological interest but also has physiological relevance. In recent years the models of cybernetics have begun to give us some understanding of how operations are combined in the solutions of problems. A formal analysis of these models reveals that their operations are also the outcome of group structures and lattice structures. Even at the very outset you find simple regulatory mechanisms, feedbacks, which may be understood as the most elementary form of reversibility, and which derive from as well as result in a complex structure. At the present time we are engaged in the study of these structures. They have a twofold interest: first by analogy with mathematical operations, which are after all, operations of thought; and secondly by analogy with the physiological structures, or, if you will, with the cybernetic models of hypothesized physiological structures.

2
WHAT INTELLIGENCE IS

In order to formulate it adequately, it is necessary at first to note that it would be wrong to confine oneself to the alternatives continuity and discontinuity stated in linear terms, as if intelligence developed linearly on one and the same level. In reality, intelligence is constructed by successive stages of equilibrium, such that the activity begins on each stage by a reconstruction of that which was already acquired in the preceding stage, but under a more restricted form. Thus, one observes in the child a first stage of intelligence, before language, under a sensori-motor form but which already takes us sufficiently far: schemes of conservation with the construction of the permanent object, reversibility with the practical "group" of displacements, objectified and spatialized causality, etc. At the following stage, which is that of representative thought and of concrete operations, that which has been acquired on a sensori-motor level needs to be completely reconstructed on the plane of representation (which covers the period two–six years) before the formation toward seven years of age of the first representative conservations and the first reversible operations. Then, toward eleven to twelve years, a third stage characterized by formal or hypothetico-deductive operations, begins by a restructuring of the concrete operations so that the new operations can be constituted as second-order operations integrating the earlier ones.

Jean Piaget, *Insights and Illusions of Philosophy*. English translation by Wolfe Mays, pp. 96–7, 115, copyright © 1971 by Thomas Y. Crowell Company, Inc., with permission of Thomas Y. Crowell Company, Inc., New York. *Sagesse et illusions de la philosophie*, par Jean Piaget. © Presses Universitaires de France, 1965.

15

If intelligence itself thus develops in a nonlinear manner by successive constructions on different levels, then the lower, or sensori-motor, level cannot be regarded as absolute and ought to be rooted in an earlier stage of an organic nature, which would then be constituted by the system of reflexes and instincts, the first only consists of differentiations starting from the more global rhythmic activities . . .

* * *

. . . Starting from a state of centration on a self uncognizant of itself and in which the subjective and objective are inextricably intermingled, the progressive decentration of the subject leads to a twofold movement, of externalization, tending to physical objectivity, and internalization tending to logico-mathematical coherence. But physical knowledge remains impossible without the logico-mathematical framework and it is impossible to construct the latter without its being applicable to "any" object whatever. . . .

3
DEVELOPMENTAL USE OF "BECAUSE" IN THE REASONING OF THE CHILD

... Thought in the child is ego-centric, i.e., ... the child thinks for himself without troubling to make himself understood nor to place himself at the other person's point of view ... (and) these ego-centric habits have a considerable effect upon the structure of thought itself. Thus it is chiefly because he feels no need to socialize his thought that the child is so little concerned ... to convince his hearers or to prove his point.

We must expect childish reasoning to differ very considerably from ours, to be less deductive and above all less rigorous ... Logical reasoning is always a demonstration. If, therefore, the child remains for a long time ignorant of the need for demonstration, this is bound to have an effect upon his manner of reasoning ... The child is not really aware of the necessity for arranging his sentences in logical order.

But how are we to inquire into the nature of logical relations of children ...?

We may begin by ... seeing how the child behaves when confronted with those conjunctions which denote causality or logical relations. ... In this connection two courses seem to be indicated. The first consists in inducing the child, by means of appropriate experiments, to make use of these conjunctions, to make him understand or invent, for example, sentences in which the required conjunctions are used. The second

Excerpts from Chapter I, *Judgment and Reasoning in the Child*, translated by Marjorie Warden. © Humanities Press, Inc. (Originally published in French, *Le jugement et raissonement chez l'enfant*. Neuchâtel et Paris, Delachaux et Niestlé, 1924.) Reprinted with permission of Humanities Press, Inc. and Routledge & Kegan Paul Ltd.

consists in noting in the child's spontaneous talk all the sentences in which the said conjunction is used. For instance, in studying the conjunctions of causality as used between the ages of 6 and 7 we shall have to note down every "because," . . . occurring in the corresponding questions. . . .

We must expect to find in childish idiom on the one hand a correspondingly rare occurrence of the "because of logical justification," and on the other a persistent difficulty on the part of the child in finding the correct justification for simple propositions which he is asked to demonstrate. This is what we shall try to establish.

Now, if such are the habits of childish thought, childish idiom ought to display a discontinuous and choatic character in contrast to the deductive style of the adult, logical relations being omitted or taken for granted. In a word, there will be "juxtaposition" and not relating of propositions. The study of juxtaposition will therefore constitute the second object of this chapter.

The phenomenon of juxtaposition is very frequent in child thought . . . A well-known example (in) children's drawing is the inability shown by their authors to portray the relations existing between the different parts of the model. The thing is not there as a whole, the details only are given, and then, for lack of synthetic relations, they are simply juxtaposed. Thus an eye will be placed next to a head, an arm next to a leg, and so on.

This synthetic incapacity covers more ground than one would think, for it is really the mark of the whole of childish thought up to a certain age. . . .

Juxtaposition is therefore . . . the converse of the process . . . of "syncretism." Syncretism is the spontaneous tendency on the part of children to take things in by means of a comprehensive act of perception instead of by the detection of details. . . . In a word, it is the tendency to connect everything with everything else. Syncretism is therefore an excess of relating while juxtaposition exhibits a deficiency in the same function. The two seem in complete opposition to each other. In drawing, children give only the detail and neglect the synthesis but childish perceptions seem to be formed by general schemas[1] rather than by

---

[1] *Editor's note.* Schema is defined variously in Piaget's writings: "A schema is a direction for responding susceptible to reproducing itself and especially susceptible of being generalized." "The schema of an action is, by definition, the ensemble consisting of generalizable characteristics of that action, that is to say of those which admit of repetition of the same action or of applying itself to new contents. Then the schema of an action is neither objectively perceptible (we perceive a particular action, but not its schema) nor subjectively, and we are conscious of the implications only in repeating the action and comparing the successive results. . . ." Battro, pp. 156–160.

analysis. In thinking, the child is ignorant of logical juxtaposition, he juxtaposes or positions instead of connecting them, but he is able to give a reason for everything, to justify every phenomenon and every coincidence. How exactly are these contradictory phenomena related to each other? This is the question to which we must find an answer.

To sum up, the object of this chapter will be first to form an introduction to the study of childish reasoning by means of an analysis of the types involved in the conjunctions of causality[2] ... , second, to draw from this study an analysis of the phenomenon of juxtaposition; and third, to show the relations existing between juxtaposition and syncretism.

I. CONJUNCTIONS OF CAUSALITY AND LOGICAL RELATIONS

The method we have adopted is extremely simple. ... We are in possession of a number of records of the actual conversation of children of different ages who were under observation for about a month each. We have selected from these records the sentences which contain conjunctions, and we have analyzed them from the point of view which concerns us at present.

... We are now in possession of nearly 10,000 remarks taken down in identical circumstances from eight children only, ... but scattered between the ages of 3 and 7 in such as to yield at least a few working hypotheses. •

The first question to be asked is that of the absolute frequency of "because." To these statistics may be added the few occasions on which use was made of "since" (*alors*) and which number 3 out of 1500 sentences spoken by Dan (age 3) and 1 out of the 1500 spoken by Ad (age 4). (The percentages are shown in Table 1.) The combined numbers of "because" and "since" are expressed in percentages, i.e., relatively to the number of sentences constituting our material. Thus 1.2% means that out of 100 remarks 1.2 contain the term "because."

Such a table undoubtedly enables us to make three hypotheses subject to verification by wider statistics and other methods which we shall develop later on.

The first is that the number of appearances of "because" and "since" increases with age and seems to increase considerably round about 7,

[2]From the translator's note, p. 61, "The reader must bear in mind that the hypotheses ... are valid *only* for the use of French words, *parce que, puisque, donc, alors, quoique,* etc. Analogous experiments would have to be carried out on English children before any objective results could be obtained as to the use of 'because,' 'since,' 'therefore,' 'then,' 'although,' etc. ...."

Table I

Percentage of Children's Sentences Involving Causal Terms and Ego-Centrism

	"Because" and "Since"	Coefficient of Ego-Centrism[a]
Dan, age 3	1.2%	0.56
Jan, age 3	1.5%	0.56
Ad, age 4	1.2%	0.60
Ad, age 5	2.0%	0.46
Pie, age 6	2.0%	0.43
Lev, age 6	2.4%	0.47
Clau, age 7	3.5%	0.30
Lev, age 7	6.1%	0.27

[a] The proportion of a child's remarks which fall in the categories of repetition, monologue and collective monologue to the total speech productions (not including answers to adult questions). (L. T.[3], p. 55.)

after having been more or less stationary just before. In other words, if the phenomenon of "juxtaposition" is defined as the lack of explicit relation between propositions which imply such a relation, there are strong reasons for assuming that juxtaposition is sufficiently present up till the age of 7 or 8 (Lev being a child 6 months or a year in advance of the normal) for it to diminish after that age. As this is a conclusion which we have already reached in another way,[3] we may be permitted to retain it with a certain degree of confidence.

The second hypothesis is that "because" and "since" increase in number with the socialization of thought, or if it is preferred, that juxtaposition diminishes as the child emerges from ego-centrism. . . . It must be admitted that the evolution undergone by Lev speaks in favor of this hypothesis; his coefficient of ego-centrism[4] passes from 0.47 to 0.27 in a year, while the number of "because" and "since" increases from 2.4% to 6.1%. But it goes without saying that the only way of really verifying it would be to look for the correlation between these two kinds of coefficients in a large number of children of the same age.

In the second place, we have made experiments in the Elementary. schools of Geneva, which consist in asking the children to invent or to complete sentences containing the word "because" or other causal conjunctions.

[3] Piaget, J. *Language and Thought of the Child.* New York: Meridian, 1955. Chap. II.
[4] The proportion of a child's remarks which fall in the three categories of repetition, monologue and collective monologue to the total speech productions (not including answers to adult questions). (L.T., p. 55.)

To do this, you begin by asking the child if he knows how to invent sentences with a given word (table, etc.). When he has understood he is asked to invent a phrase containing the word "because," etc. Sometimes the child is bored, in which case you pass straight on to the second part of the experiment. You tell the subject that you are going to give him an unfinished sentence: "Then you must make up the end yourself, so that it should go nicely with the beginning, so that the sentence should be true, etc." You then give a list of sentences to complete after the following pattern: "The man fell off his bicycle because . . . ," and the child must make up an ending. As a rule this game is quite popular to begin with. You can also take the child's answer as a new starting-point. For instance, if the subject answers, "Because he slipped," you ask: "And he slipped because . . . ," and so on, as long as it makes sense. You must at the same time try to avoid boredom or automatism.

In order to study the use of the conjunction "because" we used this method to experiment on about 40 children from 6 to 10 who were examined individually. In addition to this, we carried out a collective inquiry on 200 children from 7 to 9 by writing the sentences to be completed on the black-board. The simultaneous use of collective inquiry and personal examination is a method that has much in its favor in the experiments in question: the first supplies one with statistical data in a short time, and the second enables one to check the results by analysis. In this way we collected about 500 sentences by means of personal interrogatory, and about 2000 by means of collective inquiry.

. . . The two main types of relations which are denoted by the conjunction "because" (*parce que*), (are) viz., *the relation of cause and effect, or causal relation,* and *the relation of reason and consequent* or *the logical relation.*

The causal "because" is the mark of a relation of cause and effect between the two phenomena or two events. In the sentence which we gave to the child, "The man fell off his bicycle because. . . ." the "because" calls for a causal relation, since it is a question of connecting an event (a fall) with another event (e.g., "someone got in his way"), and not of connecting one idea with another.

The logical "because," on the other hand, denotes a relation, not of cause and effect, but of "implication," of reason and consequent; what the "because" connects here is no longer two observed facts, but two ideas or two judgments. For instance, "Half 9 is not 4, because 4 and 4 make 8." Or, "That animal is not dead, because (or since) it is still moving. . . ."

It is clear to observation that logical justification or proof appears at a much later date than causal explanation. When you ask (the child) to complete the sentence: "The man fell off his bicycle because . . . ," (he) experiences no difficulty. When you ask him: "Half 9 is not 4 because . . . ," the question strikes him as absurd. He is even tempted to give a causal explanation as an answer: "because he can't count." The distinction we are making here does obviously refer to something. It may even be said to depend upon a very universal law of mental development, viz., that the desire to check results comes very much later in point of time than the faculty for inventing explanations.

In addition . . . , it is necessary to distinguish a third type of relation, which may be considered as intermediate between the last two, and which we shall call the *relation of motive for action* or the *psychological relation.* The "because" which denotes this relation establishes a relation of cause and effect, not between any two facts, but between an action and an intention, between two psychological actions. For instance: "I slapped Paul's face, because . . . he was laughing at me." The relation here is empirical in a sense, since it is a question of two facts and of a causal explanation. In another sense, however, it is logical, since it introduces a reason, an intelligent motive as cause. We have here as much a justification as an explanation.

We have distinguished this third type because children have a tendency to replace logical by psychological relations. We gave an example of this just now. "Half 9 is not 4, because he can't count."

It was necessary to bring in these distinctions since it is our intention to point to some of the difficulties which a child experiences in establishing correct relations. These difficulties will of course vary considerably according as we are dealing with one type of relation or another. . . .

Finally, it may be wondered in connection with each of our experiments, what is the exact relation which subsists between language and reasoning. When a child fails to complete one of our sentences, is it because he does not know the conjunction, or because he cannot handle the mental relation which it presupposes? It is impossible to settle this question *a priori.* We shall see . . . that some (conjunctions of discordance), such as "although," may not be understood, even though the relation of discordance is understood when other words are used. The matter is not the same when it comes to "because." Between the years of 6 and 9, when the relation indicated by "because" is incorrect, one can always assume that reasoning has been at fault; the word "because" (*parce que*) is used spontaneously by the child from the age of 3 to 4 onwards.

. . . In the talk of . . . children, of the 134 relations shown by Jan, Dan, Ad, Pie and Lev at 6 years old, 112 were psychological, 10 causal, and 12 logical.

The frequent appearance of the psychological "because" is particularly striking. Here are some examples:

*"Look, he's laughing!—*Why?—*Because he wants to catch the apple"* (Dan). *"I don't want them to open that because it would be a pity"* (Dan). *"But Rene isn't here yet, he'll be late . . . because he always comes slowly, he plays on the way"*[5] (Dan).

"Look out there, 'cos it goes round" (Ad). *"I want to make a stove. —*Why?—*Because for (parce que pour) the heating"* (Ad). *"I must hurry up, because Mummy is coming"* (Ad).

"I'm going to sit here, because my drawing is here" (Pie). *"I say, Ez! Come here, because we'll both have the same thing"* (Pie).

It will have been noticed that the psychological "because" sometimes gives a genuine psychological explanation ("he's laughing . . . because . . .") and sometimes expresses the motive of an action or of a command ("I don't want to . . . because"). There are many intermediate forms between these two, hence the name *relations of motivation* which can be used in this connection. As a rule it is easy to distinguish between logical justification and motivation. The former always gives the motive for a judgment or statement, the latter for a desire, a command, or an act. Thus the first alone constitutes a proof, the second is only subjective motivation.

The genuinely causal "because" is rare. This . . . is due to the fact that there is very little attempt on the part of children to socialize their search for the causal explanation of external phenomena. This does not mean that they do not feel the need for explanation; on the contrary, an examination of the questions asked by children shows that at the age of 6, 18% of the questions refer to physical causality.[6]

Here are some examples of this way of relating: "(It is broken) *because it wasn't properly stuck."* (Dan). *"The train can't get past there . . . because there is too much sand up there"* (Ad). *"One of them would like to get into the nest, but he can't, because it* (the nest) *is too small"* (Pie), etc.

Logical relations number only 12 out of 134, which is a useful confirmation of the result obtained from our study of "why."[7] These relations can be easily recognized by the fact that they constitute neither causal explanations nor subjective motivations but always *proofs* or the beginnings of proof. Here are some examples:

---

[5]The sentence to be completed is in Roman type and the child's answer is in *italics*.
[6]L. T., Chap. V.
[7]L. T., Chap. V.

"No, it's a boat, because it hasn't any wheels" (Dan). *"It's badly done* (a staircase).—Why?—*Because you don't make than that way, you make them this way"* (Dan). (Dan sets out some Loto cards.) *"Yes, it's that one, since it's at the bottom."*

"How can you tell that they are going to school?—*Going to School? Because the satchel is behind"* (Pie).

It may be noticed that in some cases the "because" is not spontaneous, but is given in answer to an adult's question. Be that as it may, the problem remains as to how the need for justification develops with age. In ... Table II we shall place Jan, Dan and Ad in one group, Ad, Lev, and Pie at 5 and 6 in the other, and we shall add the results of 100 instances of "because" taken at random from the tabletalk of two adults in the course of a few consecutive days. The numbers show the proportion of times when "because" expresses a logical relation to the total number of occasions on which the word "because" is used at all.

Table II

Proportion of Times When "Because" Expresses a Logical Relation to the Total Number of Occasions on Which "Because" is Used

	Proportion	*Age*
Jan, Dan and Ad	0.04	3–4
Ad (age 5), Pie and Lev	0.10	5–6
Clau and Lev	0.18	7
X and Y	0.33	Adult

We must, of course, beware of forming any hasty conclusion from statistics which cover, it is true, nearly 10,000 childish sentences, but are drawn from the talk of eight children only. But ... our only object is to frame hypotheses which shall be tested later on by a different method of procedure. And it is the mark of a sound method that the hypotheses which guide its experiments should have been born of the crude facts of observation such as those which make up the body of the statistics given (in Table II.)

These data seem to point to some period in time—between the ages of 7 and 8—as that after which the chief development of logical justification sets in. And we shall see ... in connection with our collective inquiry that the unfinished sentences were successfully completed in a proportion of cases which increased rapidly from the age of 7–8.

If this is so, then we are warranted in making the hypothesis that the need for logical justification is concomitant with the decline of egocentrism on the one hand and with the diminution of juxtaposition in general on the other, since we have already shown that it is during his seventh year that Lev's coefficient of ego-centrism goes from 47% to 27% and that his "because" goes from 2.4% to 6.1%. This solitary but closely observed case seems therefore to indicate that the decline of ego-centrism, that of juxtaposition in general, and the development of logical justification are all of a piece.

It will be easy enough to see how this mutual dependence works out, if the sequel proves it to exist. We have on many occasions stressed the point that the need for checking and demonstration is not a spontaneous growth in the life of the individual; it is on the contrary a social product. Demonstration is the outcome of argument and the desire to convince. Thus the decline of ego-centrism and the growth of logical justification are part of the same process[8]. . . On the other hand, we saw just now that ego-centrism entails a certain lack of direction in thinking, owing to the fact that there is nothing here which tends to make thought conscious of itself and consequently to systematize or "direct" its successive judgments. It is therefore no mere coincidence that all these phenomena should group themselves around the age of 7–8, which forms a definite stage in the development of the socialization of thought.

But once again, these are only hypotheses. Let us now try to verify them by experiment.

II. JUXTAPOSITION AND THE EMPIRICAL "BECAUSE"

. . . What is to be understood by juxtaposition in childish idiom . . . is the fact that the successive judgments which constitute the child's talk are not connected by explicit relations but are simply stuck together. If this phenomenon really lasts up till the age of 7–8, we must expect to find, even at this age, that when the children are asked to complete a sentence which implies a definite relation, there is a certain amount of confusion between the various possible relations. Only this element of confusion will prove that the relation was not implicit in the child's mind, and that the child was really incapable of establishing the correct relation.

. . . And this . . . is what proves to be the case. The data show that up to the age of 7–8 the word "because" is occasionally an equivocal term which is used for all purposes, and covers a number of heterogeneous types of relation—causal, consecutive, and even finalistic, (and) the child . . . (is) apparently quite undisturbed by this heterogeniety. Sometimes there seems to be no need for the use of "because" at all; it will be placed at the beginning of a proposition which bears no relation

[8]L. T., Chapter II.

whatever except that of simultaneity to the principal proposition of the sentence. This is all the more significant in view of the fact that we are concerned here only with the "because" of empirical relation, leaving aside for the moment the logical "because" which offers additional difficulties of its own.

Here are some examples of these heterogeneous relations as made by children who are otherwise quite capable of handling the word "because," but who, in regard to our uncompleted sentences, use the word sometimes in a correct sense, sometimes in a sense akin to "in such a manner that" (consecutive relation), and sometimes in the sense of "and."

Ga (age 7), after having correctly invented such sentences as: *"There is a window broken, because a boy threw a stone,"* finishes other sentences in the following manner: "A man fell down in the street, *because he fell ill."* Now Ga does not mean that the man fell down because he was ill, but that he fell, and that was what made him ill: *"He fell down. They took him to the chemist's.—Why did he fall?— "Someone had put some ice on the pavement."* "Because" might here be replaced by "and" or by "in such a manner that." The causal relation seems to have been changed over into a consecutive relation.

Similarly, Sci (age 7;2)[9]: A man fell down the road, because *he broke his leg, he had a bit of wood stuck on* (a wooden leg)." Kel (8;6): "The man fell from his bicycle, *because he broke his arm."* Brico (7;6) and Je (8;0): *"because he broke his leg."*

Berne (6½): "I teased that dog, *because he bit me."* (Berne means: First I teased the dog, and then he bit me.)

Leona (7½): "I had a bath, because *afterwards I was clean."* "There was a draught because *the draught gave me a cold."* "I went to the cinema, because *it was pretty."* (We found out that he did not know it was pretty before going to the cinema; he did not go *because* it was pretty, but he went *and* it was pretty.)

Don (age 6): "I've lost my pen because *I'm not writing."* "I went for a message yesterday, because *I went on my bike."* "They are playing music (in the next room), because *you can hear it."*

Mour (6;10): "That boy threw me a stone, because *he is in prison."* "The man fell off his bicycle, because *afterwards he was ill and they picked him up in the street."* Of course this does not prevent Mour from correctly completing other sentences such as: "I shan't go to school to-morrow, because *it is cold."* Or "I hurt myself, because *I fell off my bicycle."*

[9] *Editor's note.* This type of notation indicates the child's age is 7 years, 2 months, and in other writings might be written (7;2). Earlier ages might be noted 1;0 (23), indicating an age of 1 year, 0 months, 23 days.

Berg (age 6) among many correct propositions, brings out such statements as: "He fell off his bike, because *he fell and then he hurt himself.*" Mor (9;1) (backward) tells us "I am not well, because *I'm not going to school.*"

Finally, let us recall the point brought out earlier, that Dan (3½) in his spontaneous language, uses the word "because" sometimes correctly and sometimes as follows: "I want to make a stove . . . because for the heating." "Because" stuck in this way on to "for" or "so that" is frequently met within the talk of children from 3 to 4 years old. One also meets with the expression "because because of."[10]

What interpretation are we to put on all this? At first sight it would seem simply that the child is hesitating indefinitely between causal explanation and logical justification. His "because" seems at times to be a genuine "because," sometimes it resembles a "since;" and the reason for this is that the child does not realize when he is being required to explain, and when to justify.

Roughly speaking, this interpretation is the true one, but it must be qualified by two additional remarks. In the first place, the child (as we have already seen and as we shall show in the following section) is in no way conscious of proving what he says or what is said to him. For instance, it is certainly not from any love of justification as such that the above answers were given to us; they are due simply to the desire to make up a relation since the child has been asked for one, and in these cases, it turns out that the first relation which comes into his head refers to the consequence of the event, not to its cause, thus giving the impression that the child was trying to justify the sentence to be completed. After all, it is the consequence of an event which constitutes the logical justification of the judgment which affirms the event. The fact that he has broken his leg is both the consequence of the fact that the man fell off his bicycle and the justification of the judgment: "That man fell off his bicycle." (The French word for since, *"puisque,"* is derived from words which originally expressed nothing but sequence *"et puis . . . que"*—"and then . . . that.")

The simplest interpretation is therefore that the child, realizing that there is a vague connection between a proposition such as "The man fell off his bicycle.' and another such as "He was ill afterwards," does not inquire whether this connection is causal, consecutive, or logical (relation of justification) but simply expresses this relation by "because."

Now, since we are concerned here with sentences to be completed and not with material taken from the spontaneous talk of the child, the conclusion to be drawn from these data is not that the child confuses

[10]French *parce qu'a cause* (translator's note).

cause and effect, but rather that before the age of 7–8 he is perhaps incapable—whether in narrative, argument, or in any of his relations with other people—of differentiating between the various types of possible relations (cause, consequence, or logical justification), and of handling them to good effect.

The best proof that this is no fanciful reading of the facts is that the same phenomena are to be found in the spontaneous idiom of children. When a child constructs his own sentences instead of completing half-formed sentences, inversions similar to those which we have described may be observed, though naturally they occur in a smaller proportion. . . . In a word, these facts are exactly similar to those which we have just elicited by means of experiment.

But it is chiefly in interrogatories referring to natural phenomena or machines that one can note at every turn these inversions due to the lack of direction in thought. For example, Schnei (4½) tells that an engine which has been lighted before him goes because of the fire. The fire is put out: "*It's not going now*—Why is it not going any longer?—*Because it has stopped.*—Why has it stopped?—*Because it* (the wheel) *is not going round fast.*—But why is it not going round any longer? . . . ," etc. This type of answer is extremely frequent between the ages of 7 and 8. It cannot be due to any desire to justify the statements, since these are self-evident. Nor is it due to any difficulty in giving a causal explanation, since the child knows the cause in question. It is simply a case of lack of direction or order in thinking; the different relations are interchangable at any moment, because they have no fixed function in the subject's speech.

III. THE RELATION OF IMPLICATION AND THE LOGICAL "BECAUSE"

Our third hypothesis is concerned with the nature of juxtaposition. It seems permissible to ask whether ego-centrism of thought does not necessarily involve a certain incoherence or, as Bleuler calls it, a certain "absence of direction" in the succession of images and judgments. If this were so, juxtaposition would be explained. Now M. Bleuler has shown in his well-known studies on psychoanalysis that a connection exists between the degree of socialization and the degree of "direction," or let us say of conscious direction of thought. Dreams, delirium, or even day-dreaming, in short, every manifestation of "autistic" or incommunicable thought appear to us as "undirected" in this sense, that the images and ideas which succeed one another in consciousness seem to lack any connecting links, any implication, even any causal relation (dreams have no way of explaining causality except by juxtaposition). Now what is the origin of conscious direction? Is it some deep and genuine disharmony? Not at all. For analysis shows that the various images and ideas which seem so disconnected are in reality grouped together by one and the same tendency or by one and the same desire. Thus there is always direction in thought, but in cases like these the direction is unconscious and is more akin to simple motor or affective tendencies than to willed and conscious direction. If, therefore, there is an apparent lack of direction, this means that autistic thought does not take cognizance of the motives which guide it. But this ignorance is precisely the result of the autistic character of thought; it is because it is not detached from the ego that this sort of thinking does not know itself. Only by means of friction against other minds, by means of exchange and opposition does thought come to be conscious of its own aims and tendencies, and only in this way it is obliged to relate what could till then remain juxtaposed. This is why every act of socialized intelligence implies not only consciousness of a definite thought direction (as, for instance, of a problem) but also consciousness of the successive statements of a narrative (relations of implication) or of those between successive images of the objects of thought (causal relations).

This, then, is how we can make clear to ourselves the connection between ego-centrism and juxtaposition. There is nothing in ego-centrism which tends to make thought conscious of itself (since this self-consciousness only arises through some shock with another mind), and this unconsciousness enables the objects of thought to succeed one another in an unrelated fashion. Juxtaposition is therefore the result of absence of direction in the successive images and ideas, and this absence of direction is itself the outcome of that lack of self-consciousness which characterizes all ego-centric thought. . . . The implicative or logical relation connects not one fact with another, but reason with its consequent, or rather a judgment with its proof or logical antecedent. The hypothesis may therefore be advanced that logical implication has a double origin, or at any rate presents two complementary features.

On the one hand, . . . before reaching the age of 7–8, the child simply has a tendency to confuse logical and causal relations. He conceives the world as being the work of a human and entirely reasonable agency (excluding, for example, all idea of chance, etc.) and he consequently draws no distinction between the causes of phenomena and the psychological or logical motives which would have actuated men if they had been the creators of these phenomena. It is therefore only after the age of 7–8, i.e., after the decline of this naive realism has set in that the different types of relations come to be clearly distinguished, and that logical implication can become autonomous.

In the second place, logical implication arises mainly out of psychological motivation; to justify a judgment is, after all, to give the motive for an act or at any rate for a certain kind of act, viz., that which consists in narrating the action instead of carrying it out. In this way the more conscious the child becomes of himself, the greater will be the importance of the "because" of justification as against the "because" of purely psychological motivation. Now we saw above that the decisive factor in causing a child to become conscious of himself was contact and above all contrast with the thought of others. Before society has administered these shocks, the child inclines to believe every hypothesis that comes into his head, feeling no need for proof and incapable if he did feel such a need of becoming conscious of the motives which really guided his thought.

To sum up, logical implication is doubly rooted in psychological motivation, whether, as is the case before the age of 7–8, the child attributes motives and intentions to nature and thus confuses causal with psychological relations, or whether, as is again the case before 7–8, the child's ego-centrism prevents the desire for objective proof (i.e., proof that is valid for all) to supplant that for simple subjective motivation.

If these deductions are right, the use of logical relations will be seen to develop after the age of 7–8 ... and analysis will show that this development coincides with that by which the child becomes aware of his thought-process as such.

In order to verify the first of these assertions, let us see at what age children are able to finish sentences which imply logical justification. We experimented on the same 180 children mentioned ... by means of the two following propositions:

1. Paul says he saw a little cat swallowing a big dog. His friend says that is impossible (or silly) because ...
2. Half 9 is not 4 because ...

Alongside of the net percentages in Table III we have placed in (parentheses) the wider percentages which contain, in addition to entirely correct answers, answers which ... show signs, ... of implicit logical justification. Later on we shall see what is the nature of these answers.

... Table III therefore shows very clearly that logical justification is a far more difficult matter than handling the empirical "because." For example, the same boys whose success was 80% (with other) sentences ... only achieved a success of 36%[11] or 47% in the case of the first of our two sentences, easy though it might appear to be. The table also

[11]Corrected, according to the original French edition.

Table III

Percentages of Children at Ages 7, 8 and 9 Who Complete the Experimental Sentences with Logical Justification[a]

	Age 7		Age 8		Age 9	
	Boys	Girls	Boys	Girls	Boys	Girls
Sentence 1	36(47)	38(60)	50(77)	54(72)	88(88)	61(72)
Sentence 2	8(41)	6(44)	30(57)	14(46)	25(62)	17(48)
Together	21(44)	22(52)	40(67)	34(59)	56(75)	39(60)

[a] Figures in parentheses are the wider percentages which contain, in addition to entirely correct answers, those which are simply incorrect but show signs of implicit logical justification.

shows that progress between the ages of 7 and 9 is fairly rapid from our present point of view. To what then are we to attribute the peculiar difficulty with regard to logical justification? The clue is to be found in an analysis of the results obtained in individual examination.

The least satisfactory answers are of the following type:

Gue (age 6) tells us: "Ernest has 4 francs. He buys with his 4 francs 2 francs worth of chocolate and a ball that costs 3 francs. This is impossible, *because he had stolen them.*"

Tacc (age 9): "Half 9 is not 4, *because he can't count.*" "Half 6 is 3, because *he divides it.*" "Paul says that 2+2=5. That's silly, because *he doesn't know how to count,*" etc.

... We need not add any more examples, though the supply is abundant. The mechanism is always the same. In the simplest cases the child confines himself, by way of logical justification, to giving a psychological explanation of the action which he is asked to justify or invalidate: "he stole it," or "he can't count," or "he divides," etc. In such cases there is still obvious confusion between logical justification and psychological motivation. In the more advanced cases the child appeals not so much to individual as to collective motives: "It's right," "You can or you cannot do that," "He is quite right," etc. But there is clearly no considerable progress; the child makes no attempt to analyze the "why" of the questions submitted to him. He invokes, not as yet a logical reason, but a collective reason, the *decus,* so to speak (a thing is "done" or is not "done"), and in this way puts logical and social rules on an equal level ... These children therefore justify their judgments in the same way as children under the age of 7–8 argue ... by simply affirming, or by appealing to authority, but never by really substantiating their statements.[12]

It is now perfectly easy to see why the logical reasons given by a child of 7–8 are incomplete. It is in no way because the child lacks the knowledge or information necessary for demonstration. For example, in the two sentences which we used for our collective inquiry it would be quite easy for the children to say with regard to the first sentence that "little animals don't eat big ones." It is less easy for them (and the statistics make this very clear) to say that 4 and 4 make 8, in order to prove that half 9 is not 4. But this does not mean that the notion of half is foreign to them. Other lines of investigation, it is true, have given rise to various difficulties connected with the idea of half, but all the Geneva children of 7, 8 and 9 know that half of 8 is 4 and half of 10 is 5, and that every half is the result of division into two equal parts. When we say that they "know" this, we mean that they know how to find half of a number, and are therefore able to handle certain notions as though they were conscious of their definitions. But this is just what they are not conscious of, and that is why, as soon as one tries, in connection, for example, with some verbal expression, to make them conscious of such definitions the attempt provokes all sorts of intellectual difficulties. One might say then that it is for lack of possessing definitions that the child can make no use of logical justification; but that would involve us in a vicious circle, for it is just this need for logical justification that causes the mind to become conscious of the definition of notions which it previously was content merely to make use of.

In a word, it is not for lack of knowledge that the child fails to deal adequately with logical justification. The reason is far simpler and lies in the fact that owing to his ego-centrism he does not realize the need for it. The examples given above show that the supreme appeal which children are tempted to make when asked to justify a statement is the appeal to public opinion. But as often happens in such cases the appeal to public opinion is always accompanied by the conviction that one is its mouthpiece; the subject is ignorant of possible divergencies, and consequently has a tendency to avoid any analysis of the reasons, valid or invalid, which alone would make this public opinion legitimate. ... In so far as they are ego-centric, children always believe themselves to be in immediate agreement with every one else. They believe that the other person always knows what they are thinking about and is acquainted with their reason for doing so; in a word, they always believe themselves to have been completely understood. This is why, in primi-

[12]L. T., p. 27.

tive arguments, each speaker confines himself to mere statement without motivation or with only such embryonic and rudimentary motivation as leaves the essentials of the matter unsaid.

Highly instructive in this connection are the justifications which we classified as "incomplete" when we sorted out the results of our collective inquiry. A separate analysis of these shows very clearly that each one contains implicity a perfectly valid reason, but one which the child cannot express, just because it is not the kind of reason which he ever tries to give. Here ... are some examples:

Maz (age 8): "Half 6 = 3, because *it has been divided.*" "To be divided" obviously means to be divided into two equal parts, but that is just what Maz forgets to say, so that he is really only repeating the original statement. ...

Bazz (age 8): "Paul says he saw a little cat eating a big dog. His friend says that's impossible, because *the little cat ate the big dog.*" As we found out by talking to him, Bazz has understood the problem, but he considers the impossibility in question to be so much a matter of course that he contents himself with repetition. Similarly, Mor (7;11): *"Because the little cat is little, and the big dog is big."* ... Even when the child has reasoned correctly, ... he cannot justify his reasoning, because he is accustomed to take the essential point for granted.

We are now in a position to ask a question, the answer to which will either confirm or destroy our hypothesis that difficulty in handling logical justification arises from inability to be conscious of one's own reasoning process. That "essential," that logical reason which always remains implicit because it is taken for granted—is the child conscious of it himself? Has he clearly in his mind the propositions "Little cats do not eat big dogs," or ... "Half 8 is 4, because 4 and 4 make 8?" It is obvious that he has not. The child has been conscious only of the particular cases to which his answer referred, and was unable to express the corresponding general laws. Now it goes without saying that if a proposition cannot be expressed, we cannot be conscious of it. When we say that the child can handle a notion before having become conscious of it, what we mean is that there has been gradually built up in the child's mind (i.e., in his various forms of incipient activity a schema), (i.e., a unique type of reaction) which can be applied every time mention is made of a little cat, or of a half, ... which does not yet correspond to a verbal expression. The verbal expression alone can bring this schema into consciousness and transform it into a general proposition or a definition. The conscious realization of one's own thought is dependent upon its communicability, and this communicability is itself dependent upon social factors, such as the desire to convince, etc.

To sum up, we claim to have substantiated . . . the hypotheses advanced. In the first place we showed . . . that juxtaposition came from the absence or poverty of "direction" in the child's mind, that is to say, from a lack of clear relations between successive judgments. In the second place, we have just shown that the incapacity for logical justification is definitely the outcome of a certain unconsciousness, an inability to attain conscious realization. And both absence of direction and difficulty in conscious realization are well known to be, if not the product (for many other factors intervene), at least the indirect result of childish ego-centricity.

. . . The study of logical justification showed that if the child is unable to give a logical reason for his judgment, even when this judgment is true in itself and correctly introduced in the context, this is because he is not conscious of the motives that have guided his choice. Things happen then more or less as follows. In the presence of certain objects of thought or of certain affirmations the child, in virtue of previous experience, adopts a certain way of reacting and thinking which is always the same, and which might be called a schema of reasoning. Such schemas are the functional equivalents of general propositions, but since the child is not conscious of these schemas before discussion and desire for proof have laid them bare and at the same time changed their character, they cannot be said to constitute implicit general propositions. They simply constitute certain unconscious tendencies which live their own life but are submitted to no general systematization and consequently lead to no logical exactitude. To put it in another way, they form a logic of action but not yet a logic of thought.

This absence of conscious realization explains why the child only reasons about particular cases. Since the schema is the only general element in childish ratiocination, and since the schema remains unconscious, the child will become aware only of the discrete objects which occupy his mind. Thus the study of "because" in logical justification showed that even when the child tries to prove his statements, he appeals neither to laws nor to general rules, but to singular and specific reasons: "The little cat ate the big dog." . . . For there to be exceptions, there must obviously have been rules.

The consequence of this fact that the child's formulated thought only takes place in connection with particular or specific cases is that we cannot speak about deductive thought as such before a very advanced stage of development. For deduction presupposes general propositions, whether these serve to characterize the individual objects with which the reasoning process is concerned, or whether they constitute the aim which the process of deduction has set out to reach. Now the motor schemas of which we were speaking just now cannot do the work of general propositions, and what prevents them is the fact that they do not confront one another in the subject's consciousness and thus give rise to syntheses and oppositions which alone would favor the appearance of logical addition and multiplication.

IV. RELATIONS BETWEEN JUXTAPOSITION AND SYNCRETISM

... We have now reached the point when we can ask what relation this phenomenon of juxtaposition bears to that of syncretism, which seems to be its exact opposite. In visual perception, juxtaposition is the absence of relations between details; syncretism is a vision of the whole which creates a vague but all-inclusive schema, supplanting the details. In verbal intelligence juxtaposition is the absence of relations between the various terms of a sentence; syncretism is the all-round understanding which makes the sentence into a whole. In logic juxtaposition leads to an absence of implication and reciprocal justification between the successive judgments; syncretism creates a tendency to bind everything together and to justify by means of the most ingenious or the most facetious devices. In short, in every sphere, juxtaposition and syncretism are in antithesis, syncretism being the predominance of the whole over the details, juxtaposition that of the details over the whole. How are we to account for this paradox?

In reality these two features are complementary. As soon as perception, even in the adult, fails to analyze an object, whether on account of its novelty or its complexity, we see the two phenomena reappear. On the one hand, because of its insufficient discrimination of detail, perception creates a vague and indistinct general schema, and this constitutes syncretism. On the other hand, through having failed again to discern a sufficient amount of detail, perception cannot make the insertions and relations sufficiently precise, and this constitutes juxtaposition. The predominance of the whole over the parts or that of the parts over the whole is in both cases the result of the same lack of synthesis, synthesis being in a manner of principle of equilibrium between the formatory tendency of the schemas and the analytical tendency.

Or rather—for the mind its not static, but in a state of perpetual movement—syncretism and juxtaposition constitute two phases alternating over indefinite periods in the mind of the child, if it be granted (as everything seems to prove) that the latter is less synthetic than ours. Sometimes the child builds up new general schemas, tries to connect everything, and tries to incorporate the new and unexpected elements into the old accustomed framework. At other times the discovery or the sudden emergence of unclassifiable and incomprehensible phenomena will burst these frameworks and dissolve the schemas until new systems are formed, only to be destroyed in their turn.

... Moreover, this kinship between syncretism and juxtaposition points clearly to the interpretation which it befits us to give to the latter phenomenon. For juxtaposition is often all the sign of the complete absence of necessity from the thought of the child. The child knows nothing either of physical necessity (the fact that nature obeys laws) nor of logical necessity (the fact that such a proposition necessarily involves such another). For him everything is connected with everything else, which comes to exactly the same thing as that nothing is connected with anything else.

4
THE TRANSITION FROM EGOCENTRICITY TO RECIPROCITY

The Development in Children of the Idea of the Homeland and of Relations with other Countries

Any psychological and sociological study of tensions presupposes some acquaintance with certain findings of child psychology. We may begin by inquiring whether, in view of their particular method of development, the cognitive and affective attitudes associated with loyalty to the homeland and initial contacts with other countries may not be at the root of subsequent international maladjustments. Even if this theory does not at first glance appear to be borne out by facts, we should next proceed to investigate why the child, as he grows, does not acquire enough objectiveness and understanding of others, or readiness to give and take, to withstand those influences for tension or maladjustment that are brought to bear upon him in adolescence or adult life.

These were the two points of view on which the survey described below was based. From the very outset, we were struck by the fact that, whilst children in the initial stages of their development, did not appear to display any marked inclination toward nationalism, a slow and laborious process in developing a faculty for cognitive and affective integration was necessary before children attained an awareness of their own homeland and that of others; this faculty, being far more

Jean Piaget (assisted by Anne-Marie Weil), "The Development in Children of the Idea of the Homeland and of Relations with other Countries" from the *International Social Science Bulletin, Vol. III,* No. 3, 1951, pp. 561–578. Reprinted by permission of Unesco.

complex than would appear on first consideration, is accordingly precarious and liable to be upset by later impacts. For the purpose of studying social and international tensions in general, it is therefore worth giving close consideration to the development and nature of this faculty for integration, since subsequent disturbances will, in the last resort, depend on its strength—or its weakness.

Admittedly, our survey covered only Swiss or foreign children living in Geneva, and, in interpreting the data assembled, some allowance should be made for the influence of the children's adult environment. But, even if we make this allowance, and pending confirmation of our findings by surveys in other areas, we are faced with a paradox which, though it may be peculiar to a particular part of Europe, is none the less indicative.

This paradox may be summed up as follows: the feeling and the very idea of the homeland are by no means the first or even early elements in the child's make-up, but are a relatively late development in the normal child who does not appear to be drawn inevitably towards patriotic sociocentricity. On the contrary, before he attains to a cognitive and affective awareness of his own country, the child must make a considerable effort towards "decentration" or broadening of his centers of interest (town, canton, etc.) and towards integration of his impressions (with surroundings other than his own), in the course of which he acquires an understanding of countries and points of view different from his own. The readiness with which the various forms of nationalist sociocentricity later emerge can be accounted for by supposing, either that at some stage there emerge influences extraneous to the trends noticeable during the child's development (but then why are these influences accepted?), or else that the same obstacles that impede the process of "decentration" and integration (once the idea of homeland takes shape) crop up again at all levels and constitute the commonest cause of disturbances and tensions.

Our interpretation is based on the second hypothesis. The child begins with the assumption that the immediate attitudes arising out of his own special surroundings and activities are the only ones possible. This state of mind, which we shall term the unconscious egocentricity (both cognitive and affective) of the child is at first a stumbling-block both to the understanding of his own country and to the development of objective relationships with other countries. Furthermore, to overcome this egocentric attitude it is necessary to train the faculty for cognitive and affective integration; this is a slow and laborious process, consisting mainly in efforts at "reciprocity," and at each new stage of the process, egocentricity re-emerges in new guises farther and farther removed from the child's initial center of interest. These are the vari-

ous forms of sociocentricity—a survival of the original egocentricity—
and they are the cause of subsequent disturbances or tensions, any
understanding of which must be based on an accurate analysis of the
initial stages and of the elementary conflicts between egocentricity and
understanding of others ("reciprocity").

We shall set forth under three separate headings the facts we have
been able to assemble; in the first section we shall study the cognitive
and affective development of the idea of homeland (between four and
five and 12 years of age); in the second section we shall analyze the
reactions of children towards countries other than their own, while the
third section will deal with the problem of cognitive and affective
understanding of others ("reciprocity").

Over 200 children between four and five and 14 and 15 years of age
were questioned.

The child's gradual realization that he belongs to a particular country presupposes a parallel process of cognitive and affective development. This is not surprising, since any mental attitude is always a
blend of cognitive and affective components (the cognitive functions
determine the "pattern" of behavior, whilst the affective functions
provide its "dynamism," or driving force, which is responsible for the
net result by which behavior is judged). But there is more than interdependence between the two: the cognitive and affective aspects may be
said to be parallel or isomorphous, since the very young find the intellectual concept of "reciprocity" as difficult to grasp as affective "reciprocity" when this passes beyond the range of their immediate
practical experience.

COGNITIVE ASPECT

We came across normal children who, until they were seven or eight
years old had none of the basic knowledge essential to understanding
the idea of their country. One boy of seven was positive that Paris was
in Switzerland because the people there spoke French, and that Berne
was not in Switzerland. As a rule, very young children, up to five or six
years of age, are apparently unaware that Geneva is in Switzerland. At
the outset, then, children have only a simple notion of the territory in
which they live (e.g., their home town), a notion comprising a more or
less direct knowledge of certain characteristics (approximate size, main
language spoken, etc.), but these ideas are mixed up with verbal notions
such as "canton," "Switzerland," etc., which they can neither understand nor fit into a coherent picture. Among these verbal notions
picked up from other children or adults, one finally becomes rooted in

their minds at about five or six years of age: this is that "Geneva is in Switzerland." But the interesting point is whether this piece of acquired knowledge immediately affects their attitude.

Until they are about seven or eight, though children may assert that Geneva is part of Switzerland, they none the less think of the two as situated side by side. When asked to draw the relationship between Geneva and Switzerland by means of circles or closed figures, they are not able to show how the part is related to the whole, but merely give a drawing of juxtaposed units:

Arlette C. 7;6:[1]   Have you heard of Switzerland? *Yes, it's a country.* Where is the country? *I don't know, but it's very big.* Is it near or a long way from here? *It's near, I think.* What is Geneva? *It's a town.* Where is Geneva? *In Switzerland* (The child draws Geneva and Switzerland as two circles side by side).

Mathilde B. 6;8:   Have you heard of Switzerland? *Yes.* What is it? *A canton.* And what is Geneva? *A town.* Where is Geneva? *In Switzerland* (The child draws the two circles side by side). Are you Swiss? *No, I'm Genevese.*

Claude M. 6;9:   What is Switzerland? *It's a country.* And Geneva? *A town.* Where is Geneva? *In Switzerland* (The child draws the two circles side by side but the circle for Geneva is smaller). *I'm drawing the circle for Geneva smaller because Geneva is smaller. Switzerland is very big.* Quite right, but where is Geneva? *In Switzerland.* Are you Swiss? *Yes.* And are you Genevese? *Oh no! I'm Swiss now.*

We see that these children think of Switzerland as comparable to Geneva itself but situated somewhere outside. Switzerland is of course "near" Geneva and "bigger." But they do not understand either geographically or logically, that Geneva is in Switzerland. Geographically, it is alongside. Logically, they are Genevese, and not Swiss, or "Swiss now" (like Claude) but no longer Genevese—which in both cases shows inability to understand how the part is included in the whole.

At a second state (7–8 to 10–11 years of age), children grasp the idea that Geneva is enclosed spatially in Switzerland and draw their relationship not as two juxtaposed circles but as one circle enveloping the other. But the idea of this spatial enclosure is not yet matched by any idea that logical categories can be included one in another.[2]

[1] *Editor's note.* 7;6 abbreviation for 7 years 6 months.
[2] Geneva is drawn as a small circle within the large circle which represents Switzerland. However, Switzerland is often thought of as a large circle separate from the small circle.

Whilst the category of Genevese is relatively concrete, that of Swiss is more remote and abstract: children, then, still cannot be Swiss and Genevese "at the same time."

Florence N. 7;3: What is Switzerland? *It's a country.* And Geneva? *It's a town.* Where is Geneva? *In Switzerland* (Drawing correct). What nationality are you? *I'm from Vaud.* Where is the canton of Vaud? *In Switzerland, not far away* (The child is made to do another drawing showing Switzerland and the canton of Vaud. Result correct). Are you Swiss as well? *No.* How is that, since you've said that the canton of Vaud is in Switzerland? *You can't be two things at once, you have to choose, you can be a Vaudois like me, but not two things together.*

Pierre G. 9;0: (The child replied correctly to our first questions and did the drawing properly.) What is your nationality? *I'm Swiss.* How is that? *Because I live in Switzerland.* You're Genevese too? *No, I can't be.* Why not? *I'm Swiss now and can't be Genevese as well.* But if you are Swiss because you live in Switzerland, aren't you also Genevese because you live in Geneva? . . .

Jean-Claude B. 9;3: You've heard of Switzerland, I suppose? *Yes, it's a country.* And what is Geneva? *A town.* Where is this town? *In Switzerland* (The drawing was correct). What is your nationality? *I'm Bernese.* Are you Swiss? *Yes.* How is that? *Because Berne is in Switzerland.* So you can be Bernese and Swiss at the same time? *No, I can't.* Why not? *Because I'm already Bernese.*

The reader can see how these children hesitate: some, like Florence, deny the possibility of being "two things together," although they have just asserted and illustrated with their drawings that Geneva and Vaud are in Switzerland; others influenced by statements heard repeatedly in their family or in school, hesitate to admit that they belong both to their home town (or canton) and to their country, and don't believe they can; Jean-Claude after first admitting it, hastens to add that it is impossible when he heard the words, "at the same time"; and Pierre, who says he is Swiss and not Genevese, can only justify his statement by an argument that applies to Geneva as well ("because I live in Switzerland"). It may be said that their real loyalty is to the canton and not to their country. But we find the same response in children who are not living in or do not even know their canton, as well as in Genevese who know they belong there. We have met children who hardly knew their home canton, yet stoutly declare they belong to it, out of attachment to their family. The fact is, that at this stage the homeland is still only an abstract notion: what counts is the town, or the family, etc., and the statements heard there; but the children do not yet synthesize these statements into any coherent system.

However, at 10–11 years of age, children enter upon a third stage, in the course of which their ideas are finally synthesized correctly.

Micheline P. 10;3:   (The child replies correctly to the first questions and makes an accurate drawing.) What is your nationality? *I'm Swiss.* How is that? *Because my parents are Swiss.* Are you Genevese as well? *Naturally, because Geneva is in Switzerland.* And if I ask someone from Vaud if he is Swiss too? *Of course, the canton of Vaud is in Switzerland. People from Vaud are Swiss, just like us. Everyone living in Switzerland is Swiss and belongs to a canton too.*

Jan-Luc L. 11;1:   (The child replies correctly to our first questions and makes no mistakes with the drawing.) What nationality are you? *I'm from St. Gallen.* How is that? *My father is from St. Gallen.* Are you Swiss too? *Yes, St. Gallen is in Switzerland, even though the people there talk German.* Then you are two things at once? *Yes, it's the same thing, since St. Gallen is in Switzerland. All people from Swiss cantons are Swiss. I'm from St. Gallen and still Swiss, and there are others who are Genevese or Bernese and still Swiss.*

It is only at this stage that the notion of country becomes a reality and takes on the idea of homeland in the child's mind. The problem is then to determine whether this development is merely the outcome of a cognitive correlation (inclusion of the part in the whole); whether the age at which these correlations are understood depends on affective factors; or whether both sets of factors evolve side by side.

AFFECTIVE ASPECT

Obviously, the child's emotions cannot be analyzed in the course of a simple conversation of the kind used for ascertaining his logical make-up. Nevertheless, though no absolute significance can be ascribed to the actual content of his value judgments, and although, in particular, the importance of affective reactions he cannot put into words must not be overlooked, it is still possible, through comparison of replies made at different ages to quite commonplace questions (what country do you prefer, etc.) to draw some conclusions as to both the type of motivation and the real but unexpressed motives. It is a striking fact that the three stages briefly described above correspond, as regards affective evaluations, to three stages in a clearly marked process of "decentration," starting from motives essentially bound up with subjective or personal impressions (of the most fleeting or even accidental kind) and progressing towards acceptance of the values common to the group, first to the family group and then to society as a whole.

During the first stage, the child who is asked for a value judgment does not even think of voicing any preference for Switzerland. He likes the country that appeals to his fancy at the moment and, if Switzerland is chosen it is for some such reason. The following are the preferences actually expressed by three Swiss youngsters.

Evelyne M. 5;9: *I like Italy. It's a nicer place than Switzerland. Why? I was there these holidays. They have the loveliest cakes, not like in Switzerland, where there are things inside that make you cry. . . .*

Denise S. 6;0: *I like Switzerland because it has such pretty houses. I was in the mountains and they were all full of chalets. It's so pretty, and you can get milk there.*

Jacques G. 6;3: *I like Germany best because my mummy just got back from there to-night. It's ever so big and far away an' my mummy lives there.*

These childish affective reactions are analogous to the difficulty, usually experienced by children during this first stage, of integrating their country, canton or town in one logical concept. The question then arises whether it is because it does not yet represent an affective reality that the country is merely juxtaposed to the canton or town, instead of being included in it as part of a whole, or whether it is because the idea of inclusion cannot be logically grasped that the country does not yet arouse any real affective response. A third solution is obviously possible: as reality is centered around their own particular doings and immediate interests, children at stage I lack the requisite logical "decentration" to conceive of their town or canton as enclosed in a larger whole; nor have they a sufficient degree of affective "decentration" to grasp collective realities outside their narrow individual or inter-individual circle: at this level, their failure to grasp the idea of their country or homeland either on the cognitive or on the affective plane, thus represents two interdependent and parallel aspects of the same spontaneous, unconscious egocentricity—the original obstacle to any integration of logical relationships and affective values.

Next we give the typical reactions at stage II to the same questions of preference or choice.

Denis K. 8;3: *I like Switzerland because I was born there.*

Pierrette J. 8;9: *I like Switzerland because it's my own country. My mummy and daddy are Swiss, so I think Switzerland's a nice place.*

Jacqueline M. 9;3: *I like Switzerland. It's the loveliest country for me. It's my own country.*

The reader senses immediately that, despite the persistence of the same egocentric statements as at stage I, the motivation is quite different: family loyalties and traditions now begin to predominate over purely personal motives. The country becomes the *terra patria*, and, though there is still difficulty in ranging the town, canton and nation in an exact order, this is unimportant: their common and therefore undifferentiated affective appeal is based on family feeling. Thus, we have here a close parallel between the inability to make logical distinctions (e.g., the idea of spatial or spatio-temporal inclusion is accepted, but not that of the inclusion of one class of ideas in another) and the inability to make affective distinctions, so that the different conceptions are reduced to a single emotional factor—that of family tradition. To be more precise, considerable progress has been made in both directions at once; we find the beginnings of logical "decentration," enabling the child to subordinate his territory (town or canton) to a larger unit in which it is enclosed; and, at the same time, the beginnings of affective "decentration" has only just begun and is restricted by the above-mentioned inability to differentiate (due to the remnants of egocentricity surviving in more extensive form in the new field of consciousness recently mastered).

At the third stage, finally, the motivations once again change and are more or less adjusted to certain collective ideals of the national community:

Julietta M. 10;3:   *I like Switzerland because we never have any war here.*

Lucien O. 11;2:   *I like Switzerland because it's a free country.*

Michelle G. 11;5:   *I like Switzerland because it's the Red Cross country. In Switzerland, our neutrality makes us charitable.*

Neutrality, freedom, a country spared by war, the Red Cross, official charity, and so on: it sounds like a naive summary of patriotic village speeches! But, the very banality of these motivations is revealing; the most general collective ideals are those which make the strongest appeal to the child. Merely to state that he repeats what he has been told at school is not enough to explain why he repeats it and, more especially, why he understands it; he gives these reasons because, beyond his personal feelings and the motives of family loyalty, he is finally realizing that there exists a wider community with its own values distinct from those of the ego, the family, the town and visible or concrete realities. In brief, he is attaining to a scale of values culminating in relatively abstract virtues, and at the same time he is succeeding in integrating spatio-temporal and logical relationships into the invisible whole formed by the nation or the country: here, once more, we have parallelism between the processes of logical "decentration" or integration, on the one hand, and affective or ethical "decentration" or integration on the other.

II

OTHER COUNTRIES

We shall now give a brief account of this second part of our investigation, considered from the following two standpoints. First of all, we wished to determine whether ideas or feelings about other countries, or peoples of other nationalities (as far as the child was acquainted with any such) develop along the same lines as those referred to in the first section, or whether there is an appreciable difference between the two types of concepts. Our second, and more important aim, was to lead up to the analysis of "reciprocity" which is, presented in the third section. For whether the child's ideas and affective reactions regarding his own and other countries develop along similar or different lines, it will be instructive to discover how, in the light of those attitudes, he arrives at that intellectual and ethical "reciprocity" which is, essentially, the faculty for social awareness and international understanding. Admittedly, the "decentration" we have just described, in contrast with the initial egocentricity during stages I–III may, in part, result from active relationships set up by the child, and in that case will necessarily lead to a certain degree of reciprocity: or, to be more precise, it will constitute an integral part of that reciprocity, of which it will be both the effect and the cause. But such "decentration" may also result, to some extent, from the pressure of the social environment: in that case, it will not automatically lead to an attitude of reciprocity, but is just as likely to transform egocentricity into sociocentricity as into real understanding. It is thus essential to make a further study—for the purpose of gathering preliminary data, and by using a process of interrogation similar to those previously adopted—of the child's reactions towards countries other than his own, before presenting him with the problem of reciprocity as such. But, in view of the similarity we have noted, from the intellectual standpoint, between the new reactions and those we have just described, it is pointless to examine separately the development of logical concepts, on the one hand, and the affective aspect of the replies, on the other hand, since the latter alone present any fresh interest.

The children at stage I are found to have the same intellectual difficulty about including the part in the whole in regard to other countries as in regard to their own, and the same judgments, based on subjective and fugitive considerations:[3]

Arlette. 7;6 (Genevese):   Do you know any other countries, foreign countries? *Yes, Lausanne.* Where is Lausanne? *In Geneva* (Juxtaposed circles).

Pierre G. 9;0 (cf. Chapter I, stage II):   Do you know any foreign countries? *Yes, France, Africa and America.* Do you know what is the capital of France? *Lyons, I think, I was there with daddy, it's in France* (Juxtaposed circles, Lyon touching France *"because the city of Lyons is on the edge of France"*). And what are the people who live in Lyons? *Frenchmen.* Are they Lyonese too? *Yes. . . . no, they can't be. They can't have two nationalities at once.*

Monique C. 5;5:   Are there any people who don't live in Geneva? *Yes, there are the people living in the Diablerets.* How do you know? *I was on holidays there.* Are there people who don't live either in Geneva or in the Diablerets? *Yes, there is Lausanne. My aunt lives there.* Is there any difference between the people of Geneva and other people? *Yes, the others are nicer.* Why? The people who don't live in Geneva are nicer than the people who do? *Oh yes, in the Diablerets I always get chocolate to eat.*

Bernard D. 6;3:   Have you heard of any people who are not Swiss? *Yes, there are the people of Valais* (Valais, as everyone knows, is one of the 22 Swiss cantons, and the child himself is a native of Valais). And have you heard of other countries too? Are there any differences between the countries? *Oh yes, there isn't a lake everywhere.* Are the people the same? *No, people don't all have the same voice and then they don't all wear the same pullovers. At Nax, I saw some lovely pullovers, all embroidered in front.*

Herbert S. 7;2:   Are there any differences between the different countries you know and the different people living there? *Oh yes.* Can you give me an instance? *Well, the Americans are stupid. If I ask them where the rue du Mont Blanc is, they can't tell me.*

It is superfluous to stress the analogies between the reactions of this stage as recorded above and those described in the first section: their concurrence is the less surprising since most of these children are unaware of belonging to their own particular country (cf. Bernard once again).

[3]We have come across normally intelligent school children living in Geneva who had reached the age of seven without having ever heard of France ("No! I don't know what that is"), but only of Savoy, etc.

The reactions of children at stage II, on the other hand, reveal that their ideas of other countries have developed in exactly the same way as those concerning their own, but frequently with an antagonism between the two types of affective ideas or reactions. Identical development in the first place: in both cases, there has been a "decentration" of the original egocentric attitude which has now given way to an acceptance of the ideas or traditions of the child's immediate environment, especially those of his family. But thereafter—and the possible antagonism originates here—the child's reactions towards other nationalities may be guided into the most varied channels, according to whether his social environment is understanding, critical, or even censorious of foreigners. Here are some instances of these acquired attitudes, the best of them shedding light on the degree of logic to which the child has attained.

Muriette D. 8;2:   Have you heard of foreigners? *Yes, there are Germans and French.* Are there any differences between these foreigners? *Yes, the Germans are bad, they're always making war. The French are poor and everything's dirty there. Then I've heard of Russians too, they're not at all nice.* Do you have any personal knowledge of the French, Germans or Russians or have you read something about them? *No.* Then how do you know? *Everyone says so.*

Francois D. 9;0:   Have you heard of such people as foreigners? *Yes, Italians, Germans, the French and the English.* Are there any differences between all these people from all these different countries? *Of course.* What difference? *The language, and then in England everyone's sick.* How do you know? *Daddy told Mummy.* And what do you think of the French? *They went to war and they haven't got much to eat, only bread.* And what do you think of the Germans? *They're nasty. They quarrel with everyone.* But how do you know that? Have you been to France or Germany? *Yes, I've been to the Salève.* And it was there that you saw that the French have practically nothing to eat? *No, we took our food with us.* Then how do you know what you've told us? *I don't know.*

Michel M. 9;6:   Have you heard of such people as foreigners? *Yes, the French, the Americans, the Russians, the English. . . .* Quite right. Are there differences between all these people? *Oh yes, they don't speak the same language.* And what else? *I don't know.* What do you think of the French, for instance? Do you like them or not? Try and tell me as much as possible. *The French are very serious, they don't worry about anything, an' it's dirty there.* And what do you think of the Americans? *They're ever so rich and clever. They've discovered the atom bomb.* And what do you think of the Russians? *They're bad, they're always wanting to make war.* And what's your opinion of the English? *I don't know . . . they're nice . . .* Now look, how did you come to know all you've told me? *I don't know . . . I've heard it . . . that's what people say.*

Claudine B. 9;11:   Do you know any other countries besides Switzerland? *Yes, Italy, France and England. I know Italy quite well, I was on holiday there with Mummy and Daddy.* What town were you in? *In Florence* (Drawn correctly). What nationality is a child living in Florence? *He's Italian.* Is he a Florentine too? *Oh yes, Florence is in Italy.* . . . Do you know any town in France? *Yes, Paris and Lyons* (Drawn correctly). And what are the people living in Paris? *French.* And are they Parisians too? *Yes, oh no, you can't be two things at once.* Is Paris a country? *No, a town.* So you can't be Parisian and French at the same time? *No, I don't think so, you can't have two names. . . . Oh yes, Paris is in France.*

It is easy to perceive the mechanism of such reactions. Whilst the "decentration" of attitudes towards adoption of family traditions may lead to the beginnings of a healthy patriotism, it may also give rise to a kind of tribal outlook, with values based on the disparagements of other social groups. In discarding his fugitive subjective judgments, and replacing them by the judgments of his environment, the child is, in a sense, taking a step forward, since he is projecting his mind into a system of relationships which broaden it and give it increased flexibility. But two courses then lie open to him: acquiescence (with its positive and negative aspects) and reciprocity, which requires independence of judgment in those concerned. Now none of the remarks just quoted give any impression of dawning independence or "reciprocity": everything suggests that, on discovering the values accepted in his immediate circle, the child felt bound to accept that circle's opinions of all other national groups.

It is evident, of course, that harsh judgments are not the unbroken rule, and that favorable estimates are accepted like the others. But even in the latter case, we are faced with the psychological problem that results from any action by the social group and, for that matter, from any form of education: is the spirit of understanding engendered by the content of the ideas inculcated, or simply by the process of exchange? In other words, if a child receives his opinions—even the soundest opinions—ready-made, does he thereby learn to judge for himself, and does he acquire the faculty for integration which will enable him, if need be, to rectify deviations and to overcome tensions?

Let us again see what are the typical reactions of children at stage III when their intellectual and affective progress seems to come nearer to independence in the formation of logical judgments and estimates and to the attitude of reciprocity inseparable therefrom:

Jean-Luc L. 11;1 (of section I, stage III): Do you know any foreign countries? *Yes, lot, France, Germany.* And any foreign cities? *Paris.* Where is this city? *In France, it's the capital of France.* (Drawn correctly.) And what nationality are the people who live in Paris? *They're French.* And what else? *They're Parisians, too, because Paris is in France.*

Martin A. 11;9 (mentions a very large number of foreign countries): Is there any difference between all those people? *Yes, they don't all talk the same language.* And are there any other differences? Are some better, more intelligent, or more likable? *I don't know. They're all much the same, each has his own mentality.* What do you mean by mentality? *Some like war and others want to be neutral. That depends on the country.* How do you know that? *I've heard people say so and you hear it on the wireless, and at school, the teacher explained that Switzerland is a neutral country.*

Jacques W. 13;9 (mentions a very large number of foreign countries): Are there any differences between all those people? *Yes, they're not all of the same race and don't have the same language. And you don't find the same faces everywhere, the same types, the same morals and the same religion.* But do all these differences have any effect on the people? *Oh yes, they don't all have the same mentality. Each people has its own special background.*

Jean B. 13;3 (mentions a very large number of foreign countries): Are there any differences between all those countries? *There is only a difference in size and position between all these countries. It's not the country that makes the difference, but the people. You find all types of people everywhere.*

But the same problem confronts us here as when we were considering stage II. Is the progress achieved to be attributed to an increasing conformity between the child's judgments and those of his environment, accompanied by a tendency to reject exaggerated views and to prefer a middle and moderate course; or is it the result of a kind of new liberation from his immediate surroundings, which favors a wider outlook? We have already observed (section I), in connection with this same stage III, how the child's mind can arrive simultaneously at a logical conception of whole units and an affective awareness of the larger unit represented by the national group as compared with the more immediate environment, ranging from the family to the town. It would therefore seem that these reactions—unlike those of children at stage II, who are apt to stress the contrast between the homeland and foreign countries—are progressing towards an attitude of "reciprocity." But how far can this be assumed to go?

The general conclusion of this section, as compared with that of the previous section, is therefore, as follows: the mastery of the concept of the homeland may be interpreted as the culmination of a gradual "decentration," correlative with a process of integration which is applied to a succession of ever larger units. But study of children's reactions towards other countries shows us that this "decentration" may take either of two possible forms: egocentricity, defeated on one plane, may reappear on another plane in the form of a sociocentricity ranging from the naive to the extremely subtle; or, on the contrary, the conquest of egocentricity may mean an advance towards "reciprocity." At this point, we should try to find out whether it is possible to assess the strength of this latter factor.

For the purpose of analyzing the understanding of reciprocity as such, while still keeping to the subject of relations between the homeland and other countries, we put two types of question to the same children, 4–5 and 11–12 years of age. To investigate the formation of logical connections, which, as we have seen, go far to reveal the stage of development of the nationalist concept, we asked each child what a foreigner was, and whether he himself could become a foreigner in certain circumstances (travel, etc.). From the point of view of affective motivations and attitudes, we put the following questions, which lent themselves to illuminating comparisons: "If you had been born without any nationality, what country would you choose, and why?" and "If I asked a little French boy the same question, what country would he choose, and why?"

On this crucial point of reciprocity, as in previous respects, we found an exact parallel between intellectual development and affective understanding. As for the formation of logical concepts, the replies at stage I reflected the notion of the foreigner as something absolute, and an inability to grasp the meaning of reciprocity, that is to say, of the essential relativity of this relationship: foreigners are people belonging to other countries (   ) [sic], whereas the Swiss (or Genevese, etc.) cannot be regarded as foreigners, even outside their own country. In the matter of affective motivations, children at this same stage thought that, if they had no homeland, they would choose their present one, but could not understand that French or English children would also choose their respective countries. At stage II, the two types of question call forth intermediate replies, showing the beginnings of reciprocity, together with obvious remnants of egocentricity; and, at stage III, reciprocity gains the upper hand in regard to both types of question.

INTELLECTUAL ASPECT: THE IDEA OF THE FOREIGNER

As we found in section I, in connection with the idea of the homeland at this same stage, a certain fund of knowledge is essential if the child is to understand the actual question put to him. Until the child knows the exact meaning of the word "foreigner," it is pointless to present him with the problem of "reciprocity," as the responses would only be something like the following:

Georges G. 6;10:   What is a foreigner? *I don't know.* Have you ever seen any? *Oh yes.* How did you know they were foreigners? *By their clothes mostly. They wear old clothes. They're always going off to the country.*

Corinne M. 6;11:   Do you know what foreigners are? *I don't know, but I've seen some. They're soldiers.*

However, once the word is understood, the question of reciprocity may be raised, but at stage I, the response is usually negative.

Georges B. 7;5:   What nationality have you? *I'm Swiss.* Are you a foreigner? *No.* Do you know any foreigners? *Yes.* Who, for instance? *People living a long way off.* Now imagine you were travelling in France, could you also become a foreigner in certain ways? *No, I'm Swiss.* Could a Frenchman be a foreigner? *Of course a Frenchman is a foreigner.* And is a Frenchman a foreigner in France? *Naturally.*

Ivan M. 8;9:   What nationality have you? *I'm Swiss.* Are you a foreigner in Switzerland? *No, I'm Swiss.* And if you go to France? *I stay Swiss, just as before.* Do you know any foreigners? *Yes, the French.* And is a Frenchman a foreigner when he comes to Switzerland? *Yes, he's a foreigner.* And a Frenchman who stays in France? *He stays a foreigner just as before.*

Marie B. 8;0:   What nationality have you? *I'm from Geneva.* Are you a foreigner? *No.* Do you know any foreigners? *Yes, the people of Lausanne.* If you go to Lausanne, do you become a foreigner? *No, I'm Genevese.* And is a person from Lausanne a foreigner? *Yes, he lives in Lausanne.* And if he comes to Geneva, does he stay a foreigner or not? *He's still a native of Lausanne, so he's a foreigner.*

Before we conclude that these reactions reflect a failure to grasp the essence of "reciprocity," two possible objections should be discussed. Firstly, it might be argued that it is a mere verbal misunderstanding:

it is the word "foreigner" and not the idea which, in this case, gives rise to confusion. To put it differently, the word "foreigner" could be wrongly interpreted as "not Swiss" or not "Genevese," etc., thus giving the impression of nonreciprocity, even though the child might actually be capable of true reciprocity. But this objection may be readily countered by the facts. The replies quoted above are, in fact, typical of a category of very general reactions up to seven or eight years of age and persisting even longer in relation to certain classes of ideas. Thus it is quite common for a boy at this level to assert that he has a brother, but that his brother has none;[4] or children may correctly put out their right or left hand, but cannot tell which is which in the case of a person sitting opposite;[5] or they may have neighbors but do not regard themselves as these people's neighbors,[6] and so on. It is no mere chance, then, if relative concepts become absolute in their minds: this is due to the lack of any power to construct logical relationships or to attain to reciprocity in practice.

A second objection may then be made: could it not be a mere deficiency in reasoning power—affecting the sense of relativity itself—and not a lack of reciprocity as an attitude of mind? There are two answers to this objection. Firstly, relativity (in this particular case the "symmetrical" character of the relationships under consideration) is the result of an operation: the deduction that A=B means the same as B=A, is a conversion operation and, from the psychologist's point of view, the operation is the cause and the relationships deduced are the effect. Any failure to grasp the relativity of a concept is therefore due to a lack of adequate operational equipment. Now the operations producing a sense of relativity are tantamount to a system of reciprocity. Secondly, the surest proof that we have to do with a deep-rooted mental attitude and not merely with logical results is, as we shall see later, that this failure to grasp the meaning of reciprocity is matched by an egocentric motivation in the values themselves.

During stage II, we find a series of reactions midway between those described above and reciprocity, as instanced by the following:

Jacques D. 8;3: Do you know what foreigners are? *Yes, they're the people who come from Valais. I have an aunt from Valais and when she comes to Geneva, she's a foreigner.*

Elaine K. 8;9: What nationality have you? *I'm Swiss.* And what are you in Switzerland? *Swiss.* Are you a foreigner? *No.* And if you go to

----

[4]Piaget: *Le jugement et le raisonnement chez l'enfant.*
[5]*Ibid.*
[6]Nicolescu: *Les idées des enfants sur la famille et le village (Étude sur les enfants roumains.* Geneva thesis, 1936).

France? *I'm still Swiss.* Are you a foreigner? *No.* Is a Frenchman a foreigner? *Yes.* And what is a Frenchman in Switzerland? *French, but a little bit Swiss, too, if he's here.* And a Frenchman in France? *He's French.*

Jean-Jacques R. 8;8: What nationality have you? *I'm Swiss.* What is a Swiss when he's in Switzerland? *He's Swiss.* Is he a foreigner? *No.* And what is a Swiss who goes to France? *He's a foreigner and Swiss, because he's Swiss.* And what is a Frenchman? *A foreigner.* What is a Frenchman who comes to Switzerland? *He's Swiss because he comes to Geneva.* And if he stays in France? *He's French.* Is he a foreigner too? *Yes.* And when the Frenchman is in Switzerland, is he a foreigner then too? *No, he's in Switzerland.*

Jules M. 8;9: Do you know what a foreigner is? *Yes, they're the people who come from other countries. There's a foreigner in my class, he comes from France.* Can a Swiss become a foreigner? *Oh no.*

Monique B. 9;4: What nationality are you? *I'm from Vaud.* What is a Swiss in Switzerland? *He's Swiss.* Is he a foreigner? *No.* If a Swiss goes to France, what is he? *A foreigner and a Vaudois at the same time.* Why? *Because the French don't know us properly and look on us as foreigners.* And what is a Frenchman? *A foreigner.* What is a Frenchman who comes to Switzerland? *He's a foreigner, but a little bit Swiss too.* Why? *Because he's come to Switzerland.* What is a Frenchman who stays in France? *A Frenchman and a foreigner.* And if I asked a little French boy the same question, what would he tell me? *That he's French.* He'd tell me that he's a foreigner as well? *No, he's French.*

It is interesting to compare these reactions with our observations on children at the same stage II, recorded in sections I and II. It will be recalled that in their judgments on their homeland and other countries, these children reflected an attitude that might be described as bipolar, if not equivocal: there is a certain degree of logical activity, testifying to progress beyond the ego-centricity of the first stage towards "decentration" and integration; but there is also a certain lack of independence, reflected in an acceptance of family opinions, thus transforming the initial ego-centricity into sociocentricity, as opposed to "decentration." Here we come across the same bipolarity, but in terms of reciprocity—the new attitude to which we should no doubt look for an explanation of the above reactions. On the other hand, the child has progressed sufficiently far beyond his immediate standpoint not to claim that a Swiss living in another country can never be a foreigner, etc.; this is certainly a development towards reciprocity. But this reciprocity may be said always to stop midway, since there nevertheless remains an undercurrent of sociocentricity tantamount to the assertion that a Swiss (or Genevese, etc.) is not exactly comparable with other people. It is surely the precarious nature of the incipient faculty for integration that accounts for this type of inconsistency.

However, at stage III, the problem appears to be entirely mastered:

Murille F. 10;6: Do you know what a foreigner is? *It's someone in a country other than his own.* Could you become a foreigner? *Not for the Swiss, but I could for others if I don't stay in my country.*

Robert N. 11;0: You know what a foreigner is? *Yes, they're all the people who are not from the same country as ourselves.* And could you become a foreigner? *Yes, for all the other people who are not Swiss, as I was born in a different country from them, so I'd be a foreigner.*

Marion B. 12;4: What is your nationality? *I'm Swiss.* What is a Swiss person living in Switzerland? *Swiss.* Is he a foreigner? *No, not for the Swiss.* What is he if he goes to France? *He's still Swiss, but he'd become a foreigner for the French.* And what is a Frenchman in France? *French.* And what is he if he comes to Switzerland? *He's French, but for us he's a foreigner.*

Pierre J. 12;6: What nationality are you? *I'm Swiss.* What nationality is a Swiss living in Switzerland? *He's Swiss.* Is he a foreigner? *No, or perhaps he's a foreigner for foreigners.* What do you mean? *For the French and Germans, for instance, the Swiss are foreigners.* Quite right. Now if a Swiss person went to France, what would he be? *For the French he's a foreigner, but for us he isn't, he's still Swiss.* What is a Frenchman living in France? *He's French and not a foreigner for the French, but for us he's a foreigner.*

Thus, as regards the formation of logical concepts and relationships no further obstacle to reciprocity is discernible at this level. Is the same true from the affective standpoint?

AFFECTIVE MOTIVATION

Although there appears to be no direct relationship between the question which country children would choose were they to lose their nationality, and whether they themselves are always foreigners to other people because others are foreigners for them, we found a striking concurrence between the corresponding reactions at the three stages considered.

At stage I, not only does the child choose his own country, but he also imagines that a national of another country would likewise choose

Switzerland, as though no one could fail to recognize this objective pre-eminence. Here are a few sample remarks made towards the end of stage I (before then, the question is meaningless, as the children are at first quite unaware of their own nationality):

Christian K. 6;5: If you were born without belonging to any country, which would you choose? *I'd like to become Swiss.* (The child is Swiss.) Why? *Because.·...* Say you could choose between France and Switzerland, would you choose Switzerland? *Yes.* Why? *Because the French are nasty. The Swiss are nicer.* Why? *Because the Swiss didn't go to war.* If I asked a little French boy the same question as I asked you just now and said to him: now look, imagine you were born without any nationality and that now you can choose what you like, what do you think this child would choose? *He'd want to be Swiss.* Why? *Because he just would.* And if I were to ask him who is nicer, the Swiss or the French, or whether they're both as good as each other, what would he say? *He would say that the Swiss are nicer than the French.* Why would he? *Because ... they know the Swiss are nicer.*

Charles K. 6;11: If you were born without any nationality and you were allowed to choose what nationality you liked, which would you choose? *I'd become Swiss.* Why? *Because there's more to eat.* Do you think the French are nicer or not so nice or just the same as the Swiss? *The Swiss are nicer.* Why? *I don't know.* If I were to say to a little German boy, for instance, "Now imagine you were born without any nationality and you could choose what nationality you like," what do you think he would choose? *He'd say that he'd like to be Swiss.* Why? *Because we're better off in Switzerland.* And if I asked him who was nicer? *He'd say the Swiss are.* Why? *Because they didn't go to war.*

Brian S. 6;2 (English): If you were born without any nationality and you could now choose whichever you liked, what country would you choose? *English, because I know lots of them.* Do you think the English are nicer, not so nice, or just the same as the Swiss? *The English are nicer.* Why? *The Swiss are always quarrelling.* If a Swiss child were given a free choice of nationality, what do you think he would choose? *He'd choose English.* Why? *Because I was born there.* He couldn't choose any other country? *Yes, France perhaps.* Why France? *It's a lovely country. I've been there on holidays at the seaside.* And who do the Swiss think are nicer, the Swiss or the English? *The English.* Why? *Because ...* Why? *Because they just are.*

It is surprising to find that, as soon as the question is understood, children at this stage voice nationalist feelings that were apparently absent in the children at stage I, described in section I. But apart from the fact that, towards the end of stage I, children begin to be influenced by remarks they pick up (as they will be to an increasing extent during stage II), a factor associated with the actual interrogation should be borne in mind: the first question asked refers to the nationality of the child questioned, and thus has the force of a deliberate suggestion, whereas in section I, his attention was not drawn to this point at the outset.

During stage II, reciprocity appears as a "symmetrical" choice attributed by the child to others of different nationality:

Marina T. 7;9 (Italian):   If you were born without any nationality and you were now given a free choice, what nationality would you choose? *Italian.* Why? *Because it's my country. I like it better than Argentina where my father works, because Argentina isn't my country.* Are Italians just the same, or more, or less intelligent than the Argentinians? What do you think? *The Italians are more intelligent?* Why? *I can see the people I live with, they're Italians.* If I were to give a child from Argentina a free choice of nationality, what do you think he would choose? *He'd want to stay an Argentinian.* Why? *Because, that's his country.* And if I were to ask him who is more intelligent, the Argentinians or the Italians, what do you think he would answer? *He'd say Argentinians.* Why? *Because there wasn't any war.* Good. Now who was really right in the choice he made and what he said, the Argentinian child, you or both? *I was right.* Why? *Because I chose Italy.*

Jeannot P. 8;0 (St. Gall) (Bright child):   If you had no nationality and you were given a free choice of nationality, what would you choose? *I'd choose to be St. Gallois.* Why? *I don't know.* Who is nicer, an Italian or a St. Gallois, or are they just the same? What do you think? *The St. Gallois are nicer.* Why? *Because I know.* And who is more intelligent? *The St. Gallois are more intelligent.* Why? *Because my Daddy is a St. Gallois.* If I were to give an Italian a free choice of nationality, what do you think he would choose? *Italy.* Why? *Because I know a boy at school who is an Italian, and he wants to stay Italian.* And if I were to ask this boy who is nicer, a St. Gallois or an Italian, what would he say? *I don't know what he thinks, but perhaps he would say Italian.* Why? *I don't know.* And if I were to ask him who is more intelligent? *He'd say Italian.* Why? *Because he has a Daddy too.* Now what do you really think? Who was right, you or the Italian? You haven't answered the same thing, now who do you think gave the best answer? *I did.* Why? *Because the St. Gallois are more intelligent.*

Maurice D. 8;3 (Swiss):   If you didn't have any nationality and you were given a free choice of nationality, which would you choose? *Swiss nationality.* Why? *Because I was born in Switzerland.* Now look, do you think the French and the Swiss are equally nice, or the one nicer or less nice than the other? *The Swiss are nicer.* Why? *The French are always nasty.* Who is more intelligent, the Swiss or the French, or do you think they're just the same? *The Swiss are more intelligent.* Why? *Because they learn French quickly.* If I asked a French boy to choose any nationality he liked, what country do you think he'd choose? *He'd choose France.* Why? *Because he is in France.* And what would he say about who's the nicer? Would he think the Swiss and the French equally nice or one better than the other? *He'd say the French are nicer.* Why? *Because he was born in France.* And who would he think more intelligent? *The French.* Why? *He'd say that the French want to learn quicker than the Swiss.* Now you and the French boy don't really give the same answer. Who do you think answered best? *I did.* Why? *Because Switzerland is always better.*

We see that while the child is induced to choose his own country (as at stage I) he is then easily made to place himself in the position of children from other countries. We thus have a relative parallelism with our observations concerning the intellectual "structuration" typical of stage II. But—and this further strengthens the parallel—at the end of the conservation, we only have to add "but who is really right?" to break down this incipient reciprocity and to bring the child questioned round to an attitude resembling that adopted during stage I. Lastly, at stage III, children show a genuine understanding of the "reciprocity" of points of view, and some resistance to the final suggestion.

Arlette R. 12;6 (Swiss): If you had no nationality and you were given a free choice of whatever nationality you liked, which would you choose? *Swiss nationality.* Why? *Because I was born in Switzerland and this is my home.* Right. Who do you think is nicer, the French or the Swiss, or do you think they are just the same? *Oh, on the whole, they're much the same. There are some very nice Swiss and some very nice French people, that doesn't depend on the country.* Who is more intelligent, a Swiss or a French person? *All people have their good points. The Swiss don't sing too badly and the French have some great composers.* If I were to give a Frenchman a free choice of nationality, what do you think he would choose? *French.* Why? *Because he was born in France and that's his country.* And who would seem nicer to a French girl, a French or a Swiss boy? *I don't know, perhaps the French for her but you can't be sure.* Which of you would be right? *You can't tell. Everyone is right in his own eyes. All people have their opinions.*

Janine C. 13;4: Choice of nationality. *I'd choose to be Swiss.* Why? *Because it's my country and I love it.* Who do you think are nicer, the

Swiss or the French? *They're just the same as each other. It doesn't depend on the country, but on the people.* And who are more intelligent, the Swiss or the French? *That's the same thing too. France is bigger, so there are more people to think, but we have our scholars and professors in Switzerland too.* What would a French person choose? *He would choose France.* Why? *It's his country and he loves it.* Whom do you think he would find more intelligent, the Swiss or the French? *That's difficult to tell. Perhaps he would say they're just the same or he might say the French are, because there are more people in France to think.* Now who do you really think is right and has given the best reply? *You can't say, as that depends on everyone's mentality, but there are all types of people, intelligent and stupid, good and bad.*

We see how, despite the inevitable superficiality of the questions to which we were forced to confine ourselves, the broad outline of this development may be clearly traced. We may thus draw two main conclusions. One is that the child's discovery of his homeland and understanding of other countries is a process of transition from egocentricity to reciprocity. The other is that this gradual development is liable to constant setbacks, usually through the re-emergence of egocentricity on a broader or sociocentric plane at each new stage in this development, or as each new conflict arises. Accordingly, the main problem is not to determine what must or must not be inculcated in the child; it is to discover how to develop that reciprocity in thought and action which is vital to the attainment of impartiality and affective understanding.

5
THE ADOLESCENT
AS A TOTAL PERSONALITY

It is surprising that in spite of the large number of excellent works which have been published on the affective and social life of the adolescent ... so little work has appeared on the adolescent's *thinking*.

The few detailed studies of adolescent thinking which do exist are all the more valuable because of their scarcity. ...

In the light of this deficit, ... we should like to see whether ... the experimental thinking of adolescents in situations which impel them toward both action and thought at the same time—enable us to set down the broad lines of this picture which neither tests nor the study of verbal (or even mathematical) thought have outlined before.

From the standpoint of logical structures, this work seems to imply that the thinking of the adolescent differs radically from that of the child. The child develops concrete operations and carries them out on classes, relations, or numbers. But their structure never goes beyond the level of elementary logical "groupings" or additive and multiplicative numerical groups. During the concrete stage, he comes to utilize both the complementary forms of reversibility (inversion for classes and numbers and reciprocity for relations), but he never integrates them into the single total system found in formal logic. In contrast, the adolescent superimposes propositional logic on the logic of classes and relations. Thus, he gradually structures a formal mechanism (reaching an equilibrium point at about 14–15 years) which is based on both the

From Chapter 18 of *The Growth of Logical Thinking* by Bärbel Inhelder and Jean Piaget, translated by Anne Parsons and Stanley Milgram, copyright © 1958 by Basic Books, Inc., Publishers, New York. By permission of Basic Books, Inc.

lattice structure and the group of four transformations. This new integration allows him to bring inversion and reciprocity together into a single whole. As a result, he comes to control not only hypothetico-deductive reasoning and experimental proof based on the variation of a single factor with the others held constant (all other things being equal) but also a number of operational schemata which he will use repeatedly in experimental and logico-mathematical thinking.

But there is more to thinking than logic ... We take as the fundamental problem of adolescence the fact that the individual begins to take up adult roles. From such a standpoint, puberty cannot be considered the distinctive feature of adolescence.. ... The age at which adult roles are taken up varies considerably among societies and even among social milieus. For our purposes, however, the essential fact is this fundamental social transition (and not physiological growth alone).

Thus we will not attempt to relate formal thinking to puberty.. ... For example, one would ... have to say that love appears only in adolescence; but there are children who fall in love, and, in our societies, what distinguishes an adolescent in love from a child in love is that the former generally complicates his feelings by constructing a romance or by referring to social or even literary ideal of all sorts. But the fabrication of a romance or the appeal to various collective role models is neither the direct product of the neuro-physiological transformations of puberty nor the exclusive product of affectivity. Both are also indirect and specific reflections of the general tendency of adolescents to construct theories and make use of the ideologies that surround them. And this general tendency can only be explained by taking into account the two factors which we will find in association over and over again —the transformations of thought and the assumption of adult roles.. ...

... Could we not say that it is a manifestation of cerebral transformations due to the maturation of the nervous system and that these changes do have a relation, direct or indirect, with puberty? ...

... The maturation of the nervous system can do no more than determine totality of possibilities and impossibilities at a given stage. A particular social environment remains indispensable for the realization of these possibilities. It follows that their realization can be accelerated or retarded as a function of cultural and educational conditions. That is why the growth of formal thinking as well as the age at which adolescence itself occurs—i.e., the age at which the individual starts to assume adult roles—remain dependent on social as much as and more than on neurological factors.

As far as formal structures are concerned, we have often taken special note of the convergence between some of our subjects' responses and certain aspects of instruction in school. The convergence is so striking that we wonder whether the individual manifestations of formal thinking are not simply imposed by the social groups as a result of home and school education. But the psychological facts allow us to reject this hypothesis of complete social determinism. Society does not act on growing individuals simply by external pressure, and the individual is not, in relation to the social any more than to the physical environment, a simple *tabula rasa* on which social constraint imprints ready-made knowledge. For, if the social milieu is really to influence individual brains, they have to be in a state of readiness to assimilate its contributions. So, we come back to the need for some degree of maturation of individual cerebral mechanisms.

Two observations arise out of this circular process which characterizes all exchanges between the nervous system and society. The first is that the formal structures are neither innate *a priori* forms of intelligence which are inscribed in advance in the nervous system, nor are they collective representations which exist ready-made outside and above the individual. Instead, they are forms of equilibrium which gradually settle on the system of exchanges between individuals and the physical milieu and on the system of exchanges between individuals themselves. Moreover, in the final analysis the two systems can be reduced to a single system seen from two different perspectives. And this comes back to what we have said many times before.

The second observation is that between the nervous system and society there is individual activity—i.e., the sum of the experience of an individual in learning to adapt to both physical and social worlds. If formal structures are laws of equilibrium and if there is really a functional activity specific to the individual, we would expect adolescent thinking to show a series of spontaneous manifestations expressing the organization of formal structures as it is actually experienced—if adolescence is really the age at which growing individuals enter adult society. In other words, formal development should take place in a way that furthers growth of the adolescent in his daily life as he learns to fill adult roles.

But first we must ask what it means to fill adult roles? As opposed to the child who feels inferior and subordinate to the adult, the adolescent is an individual who begins to consider himself as the equal of adults and to judge them, with complete reciprocity, on the same plane as himself. But to this first trait, two others are indissolubly related. The adolescent is an individual who is still growing, but one who begins to think of the future—i.e., of his present or future work in society. Thus to his current activities he adds a life program for later "adult" activities. Further, in most cases in our societies, the adolescent is the individual who in attempting to plan his present or future work in adult society also has the idea (from his point of view, it is directly related to his plans) of changing this society, whether in some limited area or completely. Thus it is impossible to fill an adult role without conflicts, and whereas the child looks for resolution of his conflicts in present-day compensations (real or imaginary), the adolescent adds to these limited compensations the more general compensation of a motivation for change, or even specific planning for change.

Furthermore, seen in the light of these three interrelated features, the adolescent's adoption of adult roles certainly presupposes those affective and intellectual tools whose spontaneous development is exactly what distinguishes adolescence from childhood. If we take these new tools as a starting point, we have to ask: what is their nature and how do they relate to formal thinking?

On a naive global level, without trying to distinguish between the student, the apprentice, the young worker, or the young peasant in terms of how their social attitudes may vary, the adolescent differs from the child above all in that he thinks beyond the present. The adolescent is the individual who commits himself to possibilities— although we certainly do not mean to deny that his commitment begins in real-life situations. In other words, the adolescent is the individual who begins to build "systems" or "theories," in the largest sense of the term.

The child does not build systems. His spontaneous thinking may be more or less systematic (at first to a small degree, later much more so); but it is the observer who sees the system from outside, while the child is not aware of it since he never thinks about his own thoughts. For example, in an earlier work on the child's representation of the world, we were able to report on a number of systematic responses. Later we were able to construct the systems characterizing various genetic stages. But *we* constructed the system; the *child* does not try to systematize his ideas, although he may often spontaneously return to the same preoccupations and unconsciously give analogous answers.[1] In other words, the child has no powers of reflection—i.e., no second-order thoughts which deal critically with his own thinking. No theory can be built without such reflection.

In contrast, the adolescent is able to analyze his own thinking and construct theories. The fact that these theories are oversimplified, awkward, and usually contain very little originality is beside the point. From the functional standpoint, his systems are significant in that they furnish the cognitive and evaluative bases for the assumption of adult roles, without mentioning a life program and projects for change. They

[1]For an example, see *Play, Dreams and Imitation in Childhood*, Chapter IX.

are vital in the assimilation of the values which delineate societies or social classes as entities in contrast to simple interindividual relations.

Consider a group of students between 14–15 years and the *baccalaureat*. [2] Most of them have political or social theories and want to reform the world; they have their own ways of explaining all of the present-day turmoil in collective life. Others have literary or aesthetic theories and place their reading or their experiences of beauty on a scale of values which is projected into a system. Some go through religious crises and reflect on the problem of faith, thus moving toward a universal system—a system valid for all. Philosophical speculation carries away a minority, and for any true intellectual, adolescence is the metaphysical age *par excellence,* an age whose dangerous seduction is forgotten only with difficulty at the adult level. A still smaller minority turns from the start toward scientific or pseudo-scientific theories. But whatever the variation in content, each one has his theory or theories, although they may be more or less explicit and verbalized or even implicit. Some write down their ideas, and it is extremely interesting to see the outlines which are taken up and filled in in later life. Others are limited to talking and ruminating, but each one has his own ideas (and usually he believes they are his own) which liberate him from childhood and allow him to place himself as the equal of adults. [3]

If we now step outside the student range and the intellectual classes to look at the reactions of the adolescent worker, apprentice, or peasant, we can recognize the same phenomenon in other forms. Instead of working out personal "theories," we would find him subscribing to ideas passed on by comrades, developed in meetings, or provoked by reading ... [H]e is motivated also to take his place in the adult social framework, and with this aim he tends to participate in the ideas, ideals, and ideologies of a wider group through the medium of a number of verbal symbols to which he was indifferent as a child.

But how can we explain the adolescent's new capacity to orient himself toward what is abstract and not immediately present (seen from the outside by the observer comparing him to the child), but which

[2] *Translators' note: baccalaureat*—a French examination taken at the end of secondary school or about 18–19 years of age. Although, in its details, the analysis of the adolescent presented below fits the European better than the American pattern, one might suggest that even if metaphysical and political theories are less prominent, the American dating pattern and other phenomena typical of youth culture are comparable "theoretical" or "as if" working out of types of interpersonal relations which become serious at a later point; thus the difference is one of content but not of structure.

[3] Of course, the girls are more interested in marriage, but the husband they dream of is most often "theoretical," and their thoughts about married life as well often take on the characteristics of "theories."

(seen from within) is an indispensable instrument in his adaptation to the adult social framework, and as a result his most immediate and most deeply experienced concern? There is no doubt that this is the most direct and, moreover, the simplest manifestation of formal thinking. Formal thinking is both thinking about thought (propositional logic is a second-order operational system which operates on propositions whose truth, in turn, depend on class, relational, and numerical operations) and a reversal of relations between what is real and what is possible (the empirically given comes to be inserted as a particular sector of the total set of possible combinations). These are the two characteristics—which up to this point we have tried to describe in the abstract language appropriate to the analysis of reasoning—which are the source of the living responses, always so full of emotion, which the adolescent uses to build his ideals in adapting to society. The adolescent's theory construction shows both that he had become capable of reflective thinking and that his thought makes it possible for him to escape the concrete present toward the realm of the abstract and the possible. Obviously, this does not mean that formal structures are first organized by themselves and are later applied as adaptive instruments where they prove individually or socially useful. The two processes— structural development and everyday application—both belong to the same reality, and it is *because* formal thinking plays a fundamental role from the functional standpoint that it can attain its general and logical structure. Once more, logic is not isolated from life; it is no more than the expression of operational coordinations essential to action.

But this does not mean that the adolescent takes his place in adult society merely in terms of general theories and without personal involvement. Two other aspects of his entrance into adult society have to be considered—his life program, and his plans for changing the society he sees. The adolescent not only builds new theories or rehabilitates old ones; he also feels he has to work out a conception of life which gives him an opportunity to assert himself and to create something new (thus the close relationship between his system and his life program). Secondly, he wants a guarantee that he will be more successful than his predecessors (thus the need for change in which altruistic concern and youthful ambitions are inseparably blended).

In other words, the process which we have followed through the different stages of the child's development is recapitulated on the planes of thought and reality new to formal operations. An initial failure to distinguish between objects or the actions of others and one's own actions gives way to an enlargement of perspective toward objectivity and reciprocity. Even at the sensori-motor level, the infant does not at first know how to separate the effects of his own actions from the qualities of external objects or persons. At first he lives in a world without permanent objects and without awareness of the self or of any internal subjective life. Later he differentiates his own ego and situates his body in a spatially and causally organized field composed of permanent objects and other persons similar to himself. This is the first decentering process; its result is the gradual coordination of sensori-motor behavior. But when symbolic functioning appears, language, representation, and communication with others expand this field to unheard-of proportions and a new type of structure is required. For a second time ego-centrism appears, but this time on another plane. It still takes the form of an initial relative lack of differentiation both between ego's and alter's point of view, between subjective and objective, but this time the lack of differentiation is representational rather than sensori-motor. When the child reaches the stage of concrete operations (7–8 years), the decentering process has gone far enough for him to be able to structure relationships between classes, relations, and numbers objectively. At the same stage, he acquires skill in interindividual relations in a cooperative framework. Furthermore, the acquisition of social cooperation and the structuring of cognitive operations can be seen as two aspects of the same developmental process. But when the cognitive field is again enlarged by the structuring of formal thought, a third form of ego-centrism comes into view. This ego-centrism is one of the most enduring features of adolescence; it persists until the new and later decentering which makes possible the true beginnings of adult work.

Moreover, the adolescent manifestations of ego-centrism stems directly from the adoption of adult roles, since (as Charlotte Bühler has so well stated) the adolescent not only tries to adapt this ego to the social environment but, just as emphatically, tries to adjust the environment to his ego. In other words, when he begins to think about the society in which he is looking for a place, he has to think about his own future activity and about how he himself might transform this society. The result is a relative failure to distinguish between his own point of view as an individual called upon to organize a life program and the point of view of the group which he hopes to reform.

In more concrete terms, the adolescent's ego-centrism comes out in a sort of Messianic form such that the theories used to represent the world center on the role of reformer that the adolescent feels himself called upon to play in the future. To fully understand the adolescent's feelings, we have to go beyond simple observation and look at the intimate documents such as essays not written for immediate public consumption, diaries, or simply the disclosures some adolescents may make of their personal fantasies. . . . [T]he universal aspect . . . must be sought in the relationship between the adolescent's apparently abstract theories and the life program which he sets up for himself. Then we see that behind impersonal and general exteriors these systems conceal programs of action whose ambitiousness and naiveté are usually immoderate.. . .

Sometimes this sort of life program has a real influence on the individual's later growth, and it may happen that a person rediscovers in his adolescent jottings an outline of some ideas which he has really fulfilled since. But in the large majority of cases, adolescent projects are more like a sort of sophisticated game of compensation functions whose goals are self-assertion, imitation of adult models, participation in circles which are actually closed, etc. Thus the adolescent takes up paths which satisfy him for a time but are soon abandoned . . .[I]n the egocentrism found in the adolescent, there is more than a simple desire to deviate; rather, it is a manifestation of the phenomenon of lack of differentiation which is worth a further brief discussion.

Essentially, the process, which at any one of the developmental stages moves from ego-centrism toward decentering, constantly subjects increases in knowledge to a refocusing of perspective. Everyone has observed that the child mixes up subjective and objective facts, but if the hypothesis of ego-centrism did nothing more than restate this truism it would be worth next to nothing.[4] Actually, it means that learning is not a purely additive process and that to pile one new learned piece of behavior or information on top of another is not in itself adequate to structure an objective attitude. In fact, objectivity presupposes a decentering—i.e., a continual refocusing of perspective. Ego-centrism, on the other hand, is the undifferentiated state prior to multiple perspectives, whereas objectivity implies both differentiation and coordination of the points of view which have been differentiated.

But the process found in adolescence on the more sophisticated plane of formal structures is analogous . . . [T]he adolescent goes through a phase in which he attributes an unlimited power to his own thoughts

[4] *Translators' note.* This passage refers to an opinion more prevalent in Europe than in America, namely that the authors' work simply demonstrates a normative view of the child as an irrational creature. In the United States, where problems of motivation are more often given precedence over purely intellectual functions both from the normative standpoint and in psychological research, another but parallel misinterpretation has sometimes been made; namely, that in maintaining that the child is ego-centric, the authors have neglected the fact that he is capable of love. It should be made clear in this section that ego-centrism, best understood from its root meaning—that the child's perception is cognitively "centered on his own ego" and thus lacks a certain type of fluidity and ability to handle a variety of perspectives—is not to be confused with "selfish" or "egoistic."

so that the dream of a glorious future or of transforming the world through Ideas (even if this idealism takes a materialistic form) seems to be not only fantasy but also an effective action which in itself modifies the empirical world. This is obviously a form of cognitive ego-centrism. Although it differs sharply from the child's ego-centrism (which is either sensori-motor or simply representational without introspective "reflection"), it results, nevertheless, from the same mechanism and appears as a function of the new conditions created by the structuring of formal thought.

There is a way of verifying this view; namely, to study the decentering process which later makes it possible for the adolescent to get beyond the early relative lack of differentiation and to cure himself of his idealistic crisis—in other words, the return to reality which is the path from adolescence to the true beginnings of adulthood. But, as at the level of concrete operations, we find that decentering takes place simultaneously in thought processes and in social relationships.

From the standpoint of social relationships, the tendency of adolescents to congregate in peer groups has been well documented—discussion or action groups, political groups, youth movements, summer camps, etc. Charlotte Bühler defines an expansive phase followed by a withdrawal phase, although the two do not always seem clearly distinguishable. Certainly this type of social life is not merely the effect of pressures towards conformity but also a source of intellectual decentering. It is most often in discussions between friends, when the promoter of a theory has to test it against the theories of the others, that he discovers its fragility.

But the focal point of the decentering process is the entrance into the occupational world or the beginning of serious professional training. The adolescent becomes an adult when he undertakes a real job. It is then that he is transformed from an idealistic reformer into an achiever. In other words, the job leads thinking away from the dangers of formalism back into reality. Yet observation shows how laborious and slow this reconciliation of thought and experience can be. One has only to look at the behavior of beginning students in an experimental discipline to see how long the adolescent's belief in the power of thinking endures and how little inclined is the mind to subjugate its ideas to the analysis of facts. (This does not mean that facts are accessible without theory, but rather that a theoretical construction has value only in relation to empirical verification.) . . .

[A]fter a phase of development (11–12 to 13–14 years) the preadolescent comes to handle certain formal operations (implication, exclusion, etc.) successfully, but he is not able to set up an exhaustive method of proof. But the 14–15-year-old adolescent does succeed in setting up proofs (moreover, spontaneously, for it is in this area that academic verbalism is least evident). He systematically uses methods of control which require the combinatorial system—i.e., he varies a single factor at a time and excludes the others ("all other things being equal"), etc. But, as we have often seen, this structuring of the tools of experimental verification is a direct consequence of the development of formal thought and propositional logic. Since the adolescent acquires the capacity to use both deduction and experimental induction at the same time, why does he use the first so effectively, and why is he so late in making use of the second in a productive and continous task (for it is one thing to react experimentally to an apparatus prepared in advance and another to organize a research project by oneself)? Furthermore, the problem is not only ontogenetic but also historical. The same question can be asked in trying to understand why the Greeks were limited (with some exceptions) to pure deductive thought[5] and why modern science, centered on physics, has taken so many centuries to put itself together.

We have seen that the principal intellectual characteristics of adolescence stem directly or indirectly from the development of formal structures. Thus, the latter is the most important event in the thinking found in this period. As for the affective innovations found at the same age, there are two which merit consideration; as usual, we find they are parallel to intellectual transformations, since affectivity can be considered as the energetic force of behavior whereas its structure defines cognitive functions. (This does not mean either that affectivity is determined by intellect or the contrary, but that both are indissociably united in the functioning of the personality.)

If adolescence is really the age at which growing individuals take their place in adult society (whether or not the role change always coincides with puberty), this crucial social adjustment must involve, in correlation with the development of the propositional or formal operations which assure intellectual structuring, two fundamental transformations that adult affective socialization requires. First, feelings relative to ideals are added to interindividual feelings. Secondly, personalities develop in relation to social roles and scales of values derived from social interaction (and no longer only by the coordination of ex-

---

[5]No one has yet given a serious explanation of this fact from the sociological standpoint. To attribute the formal structures made explicit by the Greeks to the contemplative nature of one social class or another does not explain why this contemplation was not confined to metaphysical ideologies and was able to create a mathematical system.

changes which they maintain with the physical environment and other individuals).[6]

* * *

First, we are struck by the fact that feelings about ideals are practically nonexistent in the child. A study of the concept of nationality and the associated social attitudes[7] has shown us that the child is sensitive to his family, to his place of residence, to his native language, to certain customs, etc., but that he preserves both an astonishing degree of ignorance and a striking insensitivity not only to his own designation or that of his associates as Swiss, French, etc., but toward his own country as a collective reality. This is to be expected, since, in the 7–11-year-old child, logic is applied only to concrete or manipulable objects. There is no operation available at this level which would make it possible for the child to elaborate an ideal which goes beyond the empirically given. This is only one among many examples. The notions of humanity, social justice (in contrast to interindividual justice which is deeply experienced at the concrete level), freedom of conscience, civic or intellectual courage, and so forth, like the idea of nationality, are ideals which profoundly influence the adolescent's affective life; but with the child's mentality, except for certain individual glimpses, they can neither be understood nor felt.

In other words, the child does not experience as social feelings anything more than interindividual affects. Even moral sentiments are felt only as a function of unilateral respect (authority) or mutual respect. But, beginning at 13–15 years, feelings about *ideals* and *ideas* are added to the earlier ones, although, of course, they too subsist in the adolescent as well as the adult. Of course, an ideal always exists in a person and it does not stop being an important interindividual element in the new class of feelings. The problem is to find out whether the idea is an object of affectivity because of the person or the person because of the idea. But, whereas the child never gets out of this circle because his only ideas are people who are actually part of his surroundings, during adolescence the circle is broken because ideals become autono-

[6] *Translators' note.* "Interindividual" and "social" are used as oppositional terms to a greater extent in French than in English. The first refers to face-to-face relationships between individuals with the implication of familiarity, and the second to the relationship of the individual to society as a whole, to formal institutional structures, to values, etc. Here the meaning is that the child relates only to small groups and specific individuals while the adolescent relates to institutional structures and to values as such.

[7] J. Piaget and A. M. Weil, "Le developpement chez l'enfant de l'idee de patrie et des relations avec l'etranger," *Bulletin international des Sciences sociales* (UNESCO), *Vol. III* (1951), pp. 605–621. See examples in Chapter 4, this volume.

mous. No commentary is needed to bring out the close kinship of this affective mechanism with formal thought.

As for personality, there is no more vaguely defined notion in psychological vocabulary, already so difficult to handle. The reason for this is that personality operates in a way opposite to that of the ego. Whereas the ego is naturally egocentric, personality is the decentered ego. The ego is detestable, even more so when it is strong, whereas a strong personality is the one which manages to discipline the ego. In other words, the personality is the submission of the ego to an ideal which it embodies but which goes beyond it and subordinates it; it is the adherence to a scale of values, not in the abstract but relative to a given task;[8] thus it is the eventual adoption of a social role, not ready-made in the sense of an administrative function but a role which the individual will create in filling it.

Thus, to say that adolescence is the age at which adolescents take their place in adult society is by definition to maintain that it is the age of formation of the personality, for the adoption of adult roles is from another and necessarily complementary standpoint the construction of a personality. Furthermore, the life program and the plans for change which we have just seen as one of the essential features of the adolescent's behavior are at the same time the changing emotional force in the formation of the personality. A life plan is above all a scale of values which puts some ideals above others and subordinates the middle-range values to goals thought of as permanent. But this scale of values is the affective organization corresponding to the cognitive organization of his work which the new member in the social body says he will undertake. A life plan is also an affirmation of autonomy, and the moral autonomy finally achieved by the adolescent who judges himself the equal of adults is another essential affective feature of the young personality preparing himself to plunge into life.

In conclusion, the fundamental affective acquisitions of adolescence parallel the intellectual acquisitions. To understand the role of formal structures of thought in the life of the adolescent, we found that in the last analysis we had to place them in his total personality. But, in return, we found that we could not completely understand the growth of his personality without including the transformations of his thinking; thus we had to come back to the development of formal structures.

---

[8] For the relationship between personality and the task, see I. Myerson, *Les fonctions psychologiques et les oeuvres* (Vrin).

6

DEVELOPMENT EXPLAINS LEARNING

Development and Learning

Basically, the mental development of the child appears as a succession
of three great periods. Each of these extends the preceding period,
reconstructs it on a new level, and later surpasses it to an ever greater
degree. This is true even of the first period, for the evolution of the
sensori-motor schemes extends and surpasses the evolution of the organic structures which takes place during embryogenesis. Semiotic
relations, thought, and interpersonal connections internalize these
schemes of action by reconstructing them on the new level of representation, and surpass them until all the concrete operations and cooperative structures have been established. Finally, after the age of eleven
or twelve, nascent formal thought restructures the concrete operations
by subordinating them to new structures whose development will continue throughout adolescence and all of later life (along with many
other transformations as well).

The integration of successive structures, each of which leads to the
emergence of the subsequent one, makes it possible to divide the child's
development into long periods or stages and subperiods or substages

which can be characterized as follows: (1) Their order of succession is constant, although the average ages at which they occur may vary with the individual, according to his degree of intelligence or with the social milieu. Thus the unfolding of the stages may give rise to accelerations or retardations, but their sequence remains constant in the areas (operations, etc.) in which such stages have been shown to exist. (2) Each stage is characterized by an overall structure in terms of which the main behavior patterns can be explained. In order to establish such explanatory stages it is not sufficient to refer to these patterns as such or to the predominance of a given characteristic (as is the case with the stages proposed by Freud and Wallon). (3) These overall structures are integrative and non-interchangeable. Each results from the preceding one, integrating it as a subordinate structure, and prepares for the subsequent one, into which it is sooner or later itself integrated.

Given the existence of such a development and the integrative direction that can be seen in it *a posteriori*, the problem is to understand its mechanism. This is, in fact, an extension of the problem embryologists raise when they wonder whether ontogenetic organization results from preformation or from epigenesis, and what causal processes are involved. As yet we have reached only provisional solutions, and future theories will be acceptable only if they succeed in integrating interpretations of embryogenesis, organic growth, and mental development into a harmonious whole. Meanwhile, we must be content with a discussion of the four general factors so far assigned to mental development:

1. The first of these is organic growth and especially the maturation of the nervous system and the endocrine systems. There is no doubt that a number of behavior patterns depend on the first functionings of certain structures or circuits. This is true of the coordination of vision and prehension at about four and a half months. The organic conditions for visual perception are not fully realized until adolescence, whereas retinal functioning is quite early.

Maturation plays a role throughout mental growth. But what role? We have little detailed knowledge about maturation, and we know next to nothing about the conditions that permit the formation of the general operatory structures. Where we do have some data, we see that maturation consists essentially of opening up new possibilities and thus constitutes a necessary but not in itself a sufficient condition for the appearance of certain behavior patterns. The possibilities thus opened up also need to be fulfilled, and for this to occur, the maturation must be reinforced by functional exercise and a *minimum* of experience. In addition, the further the acquisitions are removed from their sensori-motor origins, the more variable is their chronology, meaning not their sequence but the time of appearance. Maturation is only one of many factors involved and the influence of the physical and social milieu increases in importance with the child's growth.

Organic maturation is undoubtedly a necessary factor and plays an indispensable role in the unvarying order of succession of the stages of the child's development, but it does not explain all development and represents only one factor among several.

2. A second fundamental factor is the role of exercise and of acquired experience in the actions performed upon objects (as opposed to social experience). This is also an essential and necessary factor, even in the formation of the logico-mathematical structures. But it does not by itself explain everything, despite the claims of empiricists. It is highly complex, because there are two types of experience: (a) physical experience, which consists of acting upon objects in order to abstract their properties (for example, comparing two weights independently of volume); and (b) logico-mathematical experience, which consists of acting upon objects with a view to learning the result of the coordination of the actions (for example, when a child of five or six discovers empirically that the sum of a group of objects is independent of their spatial disposition or the order in which they are counted). In (b), knowledge is derived from action (which organizes or combines) rather than from the objects; experience in this case is simply the practical and quasimotor phase of what will later be operatory deduction, which is not to be equated with experience in the sense of action of the external milieu; on the contrary, it is a question of constructive action performed by the subject upon external objects. As for (a), physical experience is by no means a simple recording of phenomena but constitutes an active structuration, since it always involves an *assimilation* to logico-mathematical structures (thus, comparing two weights presupposes the establishment of a relation, and therefore the construction of a logical form). The elaboration of the logico-mathematical structures (from the sensori-motor level to formal thought) precedes physical knowledge. The permanent object is inseparable from the group of displacements, just as the variation of physical factors is part of a combinatorial system and of the 4-group. The logico-mathematical structures arise from the coordination of the actions of the subject and not from the pressures of physical objects.

3. The third fundamental factor is social interaction and transmission. Although necessary and essential, it also is insufficient by itself. Socialization is a structuration to which the individual contributes as much as he receives from it, whence the interdependence and isomorphism of "operation" and "cooperation." Even in the case of transmissions in which the subject appears most passive, such as school-

teaching, social action is ineffective without an active assimilation by the child, which presupposes adequate operatory structures.

4. Three disparate factors do not add up to oriented development as simple and regular as that of the three great successive stages described. In view of the role of the subject and of the general coordinations of action in this development, one might be led to imagine a preestablished plan in the sense of apriority of internal finality. But an *a priori* plan could be realized biologically only through the mechanisms of innateness and maturation, and we have seen that they alone do not explain all the facts. Finality is a subjective notion, and an oriented development (a development that follows a direction: nothing more) does not necessarily presuppose a preestablished plan: for instance, the entropy in thermodynamics. In the development of the child, there is no preestablished plan, but a gradual evolution in which each innovation is dependent upon the previous one. Adult thought might seem to provide a preestablished model, but the child does not understand adult thought until he has reconstructed it, and thought is itself the result of an evolution carried on by several generations, each of which has gone through childhood. Any explanation of the child's development must take into consideration two dimensions: an ontogenetic dimension and a social dimension (in the sense of the transmission of the successive work of generations). However, the problem is somewhat analogous in both cases, for in both the central question concerns the internal mechanism of all constructivism.

An internal mechanism (though it cannot be reduced to heredity alone and has no preestablished plan, since there is in fact construction) is observable at the time of each partial construction and each transition from one stage to the next. It is a process of equilibrium[1], not in the sense of a simple balance of forces, as in mechanics, or an increase of entropy, as in thermodynamics, but in the sense—which has now been brought out so clearly by cybernetics—of self-regulation; that is, a series of active compensations on the part of the subject in response to external disturbances and an adjustment that is both retroactive (loop systems or feedbacks) and anticipatory, constituting a permanent system of compensations.

It may appear that these four major factors explain only the intellectual and cognitive evolution of the child and that the development of affectivity and motivation must be considered separately. It may even seem that affective, dynamic factors provide the key to all mental

---

[1] *Editor's note.* Piaget now prefers the term "equilibration" which denotes a process rather than the term "equilibrium" which may imply a steady state, which is not a characteristic of living organisms.

development and that in the last analysis it is the need to grow, to assert oneself, to love, and to be admired that constitutes the motive force of intelligence, as well as of behavior in its totality and in its increasing complexity.

As we have seen repeatedly, affectivity constitutes the energetics of behavior patterns whose cognitive aspect refers to the structures alone. There is no behavior pattern, however intellectual, which does not involve affective factors as motives; but, reciprocally, there can be no affective states without the intervention of perceptions or comprehensions which constitute their cognitive structure. Behavior is therefore of a piece, even if the structures do not explain its energetics and if, vice versa, its energetics do not account for its structures. The two aspects, affective and cognitive, are at the same time inseparable and irreducible.

It is precisely this unity of behavior which makes the factors in development common to both the cognitive and the affective aspects; and their irreducibility in no way rules out a functional parallelism which is rather striking even in details (as we have seen in connection with "object relations," interpersonal connections, and moral sentiments). Indeed, the sentiments involve incontestable hereditary (or instinctive) roots subject to maturation. They become diversified in the course of actual experience. They derive a fundamental enrichment from interpersonal or social exchange. But, beyond these three factors, they unquestionably involve conflicts or crises and reequilibrations, for the formation of personality is dominated by the search for a coherence and an organization of values that will prevent internal conflicts (or seek them, but for the sake of new systematic perspectives such as "ambiguity" and other subjective syntheses). Even if we disregard the function of the moral sentiments, with their normative equilibrium (in which they are so near to the operatory structures), it is impossible to interpret the development of affective life and of motivations without stressing the all-important role of self-regulations, whose importance, moreover, all the schools have emphasized, albeit under various names.

This interpretation can claim to give a fairly good account of the known facts, first of all because an equilibration is necessary to reconcile the roles of maturation, experience with objects, and social experience. Then, too, the sensori-motor structures proceed from initial rhythms to regulations, and from regulations to the beginnings of reversibility. The regulations are directly dependent on the equilibration factor, and all later development (whether of thought, or moral reciprocity, or of cooperation) is a continuous process leading from the regulations to reversibility and to an extension of reversibility. Reversibility is a complete—that is totally balanced—system of compensations in which each transformation is balanced by the possibility of an inverse or a reciprocal.

Thus, equilibration by self-regulation constitutes the formative process of the structures we have described. Child psychology enables us to follow their step-by-step evolution, not in the abstract, but in the lived and living dialectic of subjects who are faced, in each generation, with endlessly recurring problems and who sometimes arrive at solutions that are slightly better than those of previous generations.

*   *   *

My first conclusion is that learning of structures seems to obey the same laws as the natural development of these structures.[2] In other words, learning is subordinated to development and not vice-versa. . . . No doubt you will object that some investigators have succeeded in teaching operational structures. But, when I am faced with these facts, I always have three questions which I want to have answered before I am convinced.

The first question is, "Is this learning lasting? What remains two weeks or a month later?" If a structure develops spontaneously, once it has reached a state of equilibrium, it is lasting, it will continue throughout the child's entire life. When you achieve the learning by external reinforcement, is the result lasting or not and what are the conditions necessary for it to be lasting?

The second question is, "How much generalization is possible?" What makes learning interesting is the possibility of transfer of a generalization. When you have brought about some learning, you can always ask whether this is an isolated piece in the midst of the child's mental life, or if it is really a dynamic structure which can lead to generalizations.

Then there is the third question, "In the case of each learning experience what was the operational level of the subject before the experience and what more complex structures has this learning succeeded in achieving?" In other words, we must look at each specific learning

[2] *Editor's note.* The following paragraphs are taken from a talk to an American audience. Piaget had outlined the factors in mental development much as they are presented here. He often refers to the American question, which is whether the stages of development cannot be facilitated by specific teachings. He reported the results of some experiments in which aspects of the stages had apparently been accelerated. His conclusions regarding the relationship between development and learning are quoted here from "Development and Learning," *Piaget Rediscovered;* A Report of the Conference on Cognitive Studies and Curriculum Development, March 1964. Richard E. Ripple & Verne N. Rockcastle (Eds.), translated by Eleanor Duckworth. Ithaca, New York: Cornell University, 1964, pp. 17–19. Quoted with permission.

experience from the point of view of the spontaneous operations which were present at the outset and the operational level which has been achieved after the learning experience.

My second conclusion is that the fundamental relation involved in all development and all learning is not the relation of association. In the stimulus-response schema, the relation between the response and the stimulus is understood to be one of association. In contrast to this, I think that the fundamental relation is one of assimilation. Assimilation is not the same as association. I shall define assimilation as the integration of any sort of reality into a structure, and it is this assimilation which seems to me fundamental in learning, and which seems to me the fundamental relation from the point of view of pedagogical or didactic applications. All of my remarks today represent the child and the learning subject as active. An operation is an activity. Learning is possible only when there is active assimilation. It is this activity on the part of the subject which seems to me underplayed in the stimulus-response schema. The presentation which I propose puts the emphasis on the idea of self regulation, on assimilation. All the emphasis is placed on the activity of the subject himself, and I think that without this activity there is no possible didactic or pedagogy which significantly transforms the subject.

Finally ... I would like to comment on an excellent publication by the psychologist Berlyne. Berlyne spent a year with us in Geneva during which he intended to translate our results on the development of operations into stimulus-response language, specifically into Hull's learning theory ... Our findings can very well be translated into Hullian language, but only on condition that two modifications are introduced. Berlyne himself found these modifications quite considerable, but they seemed to him to concern more the conceptualization than the Hullian theory itself. I'm not so sure about that. The two modifications are these. First of all, Berlyne wants to distinguish two sorts of responses in the S-R schema. First, responses in the ordinary, classical sense, which I shall call "copy responses," and secondly, what Berlyne called "transformation responses." Transformation responses consist of transforming one response of the first type into another response of the first type. These transformation responses are what I call operations, and you can see right away that this is a rather serious modification of Hull's conceptualization because here you are introducing an element of transformation and thus of assimilation and no longer the simple association of stimulus-response theory.

The second modification which Berlyne introduces into the stimulus-response language is the introduction of what he calls internal reinforcements. What are these internal reinforcements? They are what I call equilibration or self-regulation. The internal reinforcements are what enable the subject to eliminate contradictions, incompatibilities, and conflicts. All development is composed of momentary conflicts and incompatibilities which must be overcome to reach a higher level of equilibrium. Berlyne calls this elimination of incompatibilities internal reinforcements.

So you see that it is indeed a stimulus-response theory, if you will, but first you add operations and then you add equilibration. That's all we want!

7

HOW THE PROBLEM OF MEMORY CAME ABOUT

Excerpts from "Préface" to *Mémoire et Intelligence*

As we conclude this work on memory, first we confess to being surprised at having busied ourselves with such a subject, and we doubtless
owe the reader some explanation. Granting that operations of thinking
are related to transformations from one state to another, sooner or
later one must study knowledge of the states and raise the question in
this connection of the imaged representation, which was the subject of
another book.[1] But in analyzing mental images, we realized . . . that
action furthers, in certain cases, more than does just perception, the
formation and conservation of images, and this raises the problem of
memory.

We have then, in a probing way, examined what remains in memory
after an hour or a week of situations . . . (and) observed as was to be
expected that the children's memories explained more the way in
which they interpret the model, as a function of their operational level,
by what they have perceived of the objective data. But if this result was
as expected (at least from an operational and not an associationist
point of view), chance served us, when one of us encountered after six

Excerpts from "Préface" to *Mémoire et Intelligence,* by Jean Piaget and Bärbel Inhelder, translated by Sarah F. Campbell and Elizabeth Rütschi-Herrmann, pp. v–vii,
copyright © Presses Universitaires de France, 1968. Reprinted by permission of Presses
Universitaires de France, Paris, and Routledge & Kegan Paul Ltd., London.

[1]J. Piaget and B. Inhelder, *L'image mentale chez l'enfant.* Presses Universitaires de
France, 1966.

months one of the subjects whom he had questioned before and whom he asked, before giving a new test, if he remembered the earlier presentation. Then, this child recalled it, which was nice, but with a more advanced schematization. Here then was a problem: if, in long-term memory, recollection had to suffer deterioration or at best is just conserved, the operational schemes could, on the contrary, in the course of development, be only maintained or advance. Would we have, in this case, to admit that recollections would follow their destiny or their own course, without relation to intelligence, or that, according to the situations (simple or conflicting) and the levels of development (far from or close to the solution of the implied problem) memory would depend upon the operational schemes, in being able then to lead either to systematic deformations but which are understandable by the mechanisms of schemes, or paradoxically to ameliorations of the content of memory due to progress of intelligence itself? The reader will notice that all our results are oriented in the direction of this interaction between memory and intelligence: at times there is spectacular progress in responding between one week and six months without new presentation of the model (as in the memory of serial configurations . . .), at other times there are deforming schematizations intended to resolve conflict (as between numerical correspondences and spatial sizes . . .), etc.

Since the problem of memory is now the order of the day, we thus risk some general considerations on the correspondences between the figural element of memory (from perceptual recognition to memory images) and the operational elements (schemes of intelligence, the conservation of which goes beyond what we ordinarily call memory in the strict sense): the structuring necessary for memorial retention seems, in effect, systematic and even required in a biological sense, if as we tend to admit, memory implies the integration of RNA which itself possesses structure. On the other hand, we have been led to insist on the fundamental importance of a mnemonic stage which we call memory of reconstruction and which is wedged between the elementary level of simple recognition and the higher level of recall.

Briefly, one will find in this book a certain number of experimental facts, as well as several theoretical attempts which only the future will determine as venturesome or sound. Whichever of these turns out, there is one aspect of this research which reassures and encourages us: that is to discover with astonishing precision, in an area which could have been considered as very far removed from the mechanism of cognitive operations, the unfolding of operational stages just as in the detail of the levels on whose existence we could have held some reservations, from reading the works of critics who do not believe, or not yet, in operation. . . .

ABOUT FEELINGS, "WILL AND ACTION"

Will and Action

I once heard in a bus, two bus conductors saying about a third person, "He is a nice man; he is loyal; he is logical." What did they mean by saying "He is logical"? Certainly not that in his reasoning he was conforming to Aristotelian logic, but simply that he was coherent in his attitudes, in his affective reactions, and consequently one could depend on him. It is this kind of coherence that I call the logic of feelings.

A sociologist, Georges Vaucher, in his interesting book on judgment of values, discusses a logic of feelings. He maintains that we cannot talk of logic of feelings in the same sense that we talk about cognitive logic, because feelings are not conserved, they are transformed and are submitted to indefinite fluctuations. In the logic of cognition, Vaucher says, the terms in which we reason must be conserved, otherwise reasoning would not be possible. For example, when one says that A = B, B = C, therefore A = C, A and C are the equal at the beginning and at the end of the reasoning. However, once you start comparing and manipulating feelings, according to Vaucher, you transform them just by the plain fact of examining them. Therefore, he says, a logic of feelings does not exist.

Jean Piaget, "*Will and Action,*" Reprinted with permission from the *Bulletin of the Menninger Clinic, Vol. 26,* No. 3, pp. 138–145, copyright © 1962 by the Menninger Foundation.

Vaucher, in his argument, refers only to those spontaneous feelings that are characteristic of the second stage in the evolution of affective life; of spontaneous sympathy and antipathy which in fact may appear, disappear, and fluctuate in different ways. There is, however, a conservation of feelings and of affective values; it is that imposed by the moral feelings.

Take, for example, the feeling of gratitude. Insofar as this feeling is spontaneous, it fluctuates. We all know how gratitude is easily forgotten. But when I am asked a favor by someone who was of service to me once, and I have forgotten the gratitude that I felt toward him, I will remember this gratitude. Besides being spontaneous, the gratitude will then become a moral persuasion, and the plain fact that it becomes a moral feeling, shows that there is here a compelled conservation, something analogous to logical conservation. It is the same way with feelings of justice. Treating everybody the same way, equally, compels a certain conservation of values; it is the same with moral feelings based on reciprocity.

In other words, morality as a whole is an apparatus of conservation of affective values, by means of obligations, and there we have something analogous to cognitive conservations.

But can we go a little further and ask ourselves if there exists in the affective field, something that could be equivalent to the operations of thought as such? Thought operations are internalized actions, actions which have become reversible and which are coordinated with other operations in structures which themselves are reversible. I think that there exists such an operation in the affective field, an affective operation. This affective operation is what we call will, and it is the problem of will that I propose to discuss.

I shall start by examining the different definitions of will that have been given. There were a great number of old definitions which, for my part, were all insufficient and even profoundly insufficient, until William James discussed the problem of will in more precise terms. The old definitions confuse will with different affective tendencies. For example, Condillac defined will as desire. If this were the case, one does not need the term will. Why have two words to describe the same thing? Wundt and Ribot considered as will, the element of tendency in the affective life. According to Wundt, the will is all that tends to prolong a feeling. There is something true there, and that is the tendency to conserve. But that is not enough; not all tendencies constitute an act of will. Other authors, like Bergson, Müller-Freienfels, Warren, and others, have defined the will by the personality; it is what engages the personality as a whole. This is completely false.

James has shown that when there is an act of will, when the will intervenes in our action, the personality is divided. There is a conflict there; without this conflict, there could be no need for will. So I cannot see how you can define the will by the whole personality. Rignano went a step further by suspecting what James finally showed, that is to say, that when will intervenes, you must consider two tendencies. Rignano defines will as an intention, but an intention that refers to the future, rather than an intention that bears on the present, such as a simple tendency or a simple desire. This definition is better than the others given, but it does not seem sufficient because the tendency that refers to the future may simply be a question of premeditated interest. For example, during a dinner, knowing the menu, I do not take soup because I want to save my appetite for the main dish that follows. In this case, a present tendency is subordinated to a tendency that bears on the future, but according to Rignano's definition, this is not an act of will, it is simply a question of interest.

Finally, the problem was discussed in an enlightening way by James. For James there is will only when there is a conflict of tendencies; without this conflict, will would be confused with desire, with simple tendencies, and it would be useless as a separate function. So, in case of conflict, says James, we are confronted with an initial situation in which we find two tendencies: On one hand is a tendency which initially is strong and which corresponds to the actual desire of the individual, and on the other hand is a tendency that initially is weak, which does not correspond to the actual desire of the individual but to some tendencies of a higher level, for example, to a duty or to a value judged by him superior to his actual desire. An act of will, then, consists in reversing the situation, that is to say, in reinforcing the weak tendency and in thwarting the initially strong desire. In this way, after the act of the will, the weak tendency has become strong and the strong desire of the beginning has been defeated by the initially weaker tendency. For example:

"I am at my desk and I am in the process of preparing a lecture; outside it is beautiful weather and I feel like walking. The strong tendency is my actual desire to leave my work and go out in the sun for a walk; the weak tendency is to continue my work, a tendency that corresponds to something like a duty, like a moral obligation. In fact, it is something that I simply have to do, while the other is a desire to do so. If I yield to my actual desire, that is to say, if I leave my work and go for a walk, we cannot say that there is there an act of will; we can say that there is simply a realization of my desire. On the contrary, if I succeed in resisting this tendency, if I continue to work, even though I have a great desire to go out in the sun, in other words, if the initially weak tendency ends by removing the strong tendency, then we can talk of will; the will has triumphed over the desire."

James gives an excellent description, but there is no general explanation. This description brings up a problem. From the moment this initially weak tendency becomes stronger, an additional force has been added. Where does this force come from? James leaves the problem open and states precisely that he does not give an explanation, but only a description of the problem. To describe this additional force, this reversal of force, he speaks of a "fiat," of a creative act, to show precisely that it is not an explanation and that there is a certain mystery about it.

Binet criticized James' theory in the *Année Psychologique,* in which he asked: "Where does this additional force come from?" It is there the problem of will lies.

Charles Blondel has offered a solution, in a chapter on will, in his dissertation on the psychology of Dumas. Blondel says that it is impossible to solve the problem of the will if you look at it only through the psychology of the individual; it seems like a mystery. There is a reversal of the strength of the tendencies, which cannot be explained without assuming an additional force and no one understands where this additional force comes from, if one considers the individual only. On the contrary, if we examined will from the collective or social point of view, then, according to Blondel, there is a possible solution. Social life, in fact, imposes on us collective imperatives, orders, duties that would be discussed psychoanalytically in terms of superego. Blondel, a sociologist, talks about collective imperatives.

The additional force of James, says Blondel, is precisely the collective imperatives. The individual has no will of his own; the will is the collective imperatives, it is the moral values that the society has imposed on the individual, that canalize his behavior, that allow him to bypass his desire of the moment. This is the kind of solution that Blondel proposes and which is similar to other sociological solutions.

But, so far as I am concerned, Blondel's is not a solution of the psychological problem of will. In fact, if the collective imperative, or the superego, if you prefer, is strong enough, there is no need for will; there are going to be no conflicts, the individual is always going to submit to the rules that dominate him. If, on the contrary, there is conflict, it is because at the beginning the collective imperative is weaker than the desire, the desire is momentarily stronger than the collective imperative, and the act of the will is in reversing the situation, that is to say, in rendering to the collective imperative its strength which was momentarily lost. In Blondel's explanation, as in James' description, we need an additional force; and again we cannot understand where this force comes from. The solution that Blondel offers is not a solution, as far as I am concerned.

I shall now try to deal with the problem of will by showing two things: first, that the problem of will is analogous to that of the operations of intelligence; with the only difference that it is an affective operation and deals with values, actions, or decisions. Second, I should like to show that there is no need here of an additional force, that the problem of the additional force comes simply from the fact of reasoning in terms of absolute forces, of absolute values; but if we look at will from the point of view of relative values, as we have to do in the perceptual field, for example, the problem disappears.

First, look at the analogy between the will and the operation of intelligence. We find the exact equivalent of the conflict of tendencies that James has described, whenever a logical operation is in conflict with a tendency that is momentarily stronger, a tendency, for example, related to a perceptual configuration. Take the experiment with children concerning the conservation of number at the beginning of the stage of concrete operations, in which the first two rows of coins are equivalent by virtue of visual correspondence.

If we enlarge one row, the child finds himself in conflict. At the beginning there is an inferior tendency which is strong: It is the tendency of judging according to the configuration; there is a longer row, and consequently there will be more elements in that than in the shorter row; there is no conservation. There is also a tendency of superior order, but weaker, which consists in conserving the equality not by virtue of a perceptual verification, which is strong, but simply by virtue of reasoning, which is weak.

How does a superior tendency, initially weaker, end by triumphing, by removing the inferior perceptual tendency which at the beginning is the stronger? What happens is that the superior tendency carries away the inferior one by an act of decentration, it carries it away from the moment the child is subordinating the actual perceptive tendency to a system of transformations. The superior tendency removes the inferior one from the moment that there is decentration and reversibility, that is to say, from the moment the child is capable of remembering what precedes, from the moment he is capable of coming back, of remembering that there was an optical equality of the rows of coins and that all that one did was to change their spacing. In the other direction, from the moment the child is capable of anticipating what can follow, of foreseeing that one can also space the other row and achieve again an optical equality. So there is decentration when the actual configuration is subordinated to previous as well as to future configurations and especially to transformations that relate these configurations to one another. So here the problem is exactly parallel and the inferior tendency becomes strong simply by decentration and reversibility.

Well, I maintain that exactly the same thing takes place in the act of will. Why is it that the tendency, the actual inferior desire is stronger at the beginning? It is simply because one forgets to think of the past or of the future; it is simply because one lives in the present, because he is situated in the actual perceptual configuration: I am in front of my desk; I have no particular desire to work; I see the sun outside; I feel like walking. It is the actual perceptual configuration that carries me away over everything else; if I give in to my desire, it is simply that I stayed in the present and did not think either of the past or of the future.

Why did the initially weak tendency to continue my work end by being the stronger? Because, in this case, there is decentration: I can free myself of the actual desire in two ways, but it is always by calling upon the conservation of values. I can free myself then by a double act of reversibility: either I recall the past, or I anticipate the future. I recall the past, that is to say that I am engaged, that the work has to be finished and I have to do my work. Or, on the contrary, I anticipate the future, I anticipate the satisfaction that this work will give me when accomplished, what I am going to feel when I will no longer be engaged in this task which is not particularly pleasant to me. Therefore, the act of will consists here simply in relying upon a decentration, upon something which is exactly analogous to the reversibility of the intellectual operation and which consists in subordinating the actual value, the desire, to a larger scale of values, the value of the engagement that I have undertaken, the value of the work. From the moment that I react according to my ordinary scale of values, from the moment that I include my actual desire in the permanent scale of values, the conflict is resolved and the initially strong tendency becomes the weaker one.

The will is, therefore, it seems to me, exactly parallel to an intellectual operation except that it is an affective operation that bears only on the conservation and coordination of values, and on reversibility in the domain of values, while the intellectual operation bears on the coordination and the conservation of verifications, or of relations.

What about the problem of the additional force? There is no need for an additional force because the force of the initial tendency, which was momentarily the stronger, is but a relative force: This tendency was stronger simply because we plunged into the actual configuration, forgetting the past and the future, and therefore forgetting the permanent scale of values. So we have to do here with a restricted configuration and it is within this restricted configuration that the force, the desire, carries away the other tendency. On the contrary, once the act of decentration and reversibility intervenes, this force diminishes, but not absolutely; it diminishes only in a relative sense, relative to the values that we had forgotten, which regain their force and then modify the force of the actual configuration. In other words, the problem of the additional force in the domain of the will must be put in terms analogous to those of perceptual values and not in terms of absolute forces.

Perceptually, when we compare sizes, if B compared to A is smaller, or B is bigger in comparison with C, B will be then overestimated in relation to A, and underestimated in relation to C; B will change value according to the context. There is no constant absolute value, there are only relative values. With the decentration, on the contrary (perceptive or intellectual), we arrive at a certain conservation of these sizes, of these values. It is exactly the same in the affective field. As long as we are in the actual configuration, the momentarily strong desire is strong as related to what we forget. On the contrary, from the moment that it is replaced in the permanent scale of values, its relative value diminishes. Therefore, the problem of the additional force does not exist; it is a pseudo problem, because it is put in terms of absolute values.

I conclude this exposition: having will is to possess a permanent scale of values. If we possess a permanent scale of values, the conflicts can be resolved, the solution of the conflicts consisting in a subordination of the actual situation to permanent values. And conversely, not having will, means knowing only unstable and momentary values, not being able to rely upon a permanent scale of values. Will is then comparable in this respect to affective operations of coordination and conservation of values. But I would like to specify that this is not an intellectualistic interpretation of will, but an affective operation, by which I mean that it is not enough to remember, to know, to understand. If I am at my desk and recall my obligations, which I invoke simply through intelligence, and the satisfaction that I will have when I finish this work, my desire will not change as long as my understanding is only through intelligence. To decentrate in the domain of will is not to invoke memories through the intelligence, but to revive permanent values, that is to say, to reanimate permanent values, to feel them, which means that it is an affective operation and not an intellectual one.

A final point, which might answer the objection that in order to decentrate, one must call upon an additional force, that one must have will in order to decentrate. But what is this decentration? Like all affective regulations, it is a regulation of effort when one is interested in his work, or a regulation of fatigue in case of disinterest or depression. The force of the regulation is something common to all affective regulations. So in this particular case, the force necessary for this regulation is not a new force, it is a force which results directly from the permanent scale of values. If these values are strong, then the regulation will result directly without the problem of adding a new force. And if these values are weak or incoherent, there will be no will.

9
A FEEDBACK MODEL OF COGNITIVE FUNCTIONING

The Problem of Memory and Its Place in Cognitive Functions

As opposed to perception, which is the apprehending of immediate and present data *(hic and nunc)*, memory may appear to be simply an almost direct understanding of what has been acquired or experienced in the past. The most elementary form of memory, which is recognition, would then seem to consist of only two elements: a perception, on the one hand, and an analogous recognition on the other. This sort of memory comes down to being the simple conservation of whatever component belonged to the earlier perception.

But right away these assumptions raise a world of problems. First, the reaction to immediate and present data is not only perceptual, and perception itself (which is an organization of sensory data) constitutes several levels of distinct structurations. Perception is not a simple registration, since it is also identification or assimilation, which constitutes a schematism: when the subject recognizes an object he had perceived earlier, does that recognition constitute then a memory or a conservation of the perceptual schemes, and in what form, or from only sensory data organized by them, and, anew, in what form? Further, all perception is prolonged in interpretations by assimilation to whatever sensory-motor schemes (action schemes), either conceptual and representative, preoperational or operational, and it is clear that memory involves these interpretations or meanings of a rank higher than perceptions as well as the earlier perceptions themselves.

One would then come to see from analysis of these elementary cases in memory a certain actualization implying a conservation of all the past, or at least of everything in the subject's past which is useful in his present actions or knowledge. But then the problem of mnemonic processes is enlarged indefinitely, or if, to understand them, we have to have recourse in principle to a conservation of all the past, how could we explain this conservation and how separate out in this past what effectively lies at the heart of these particular facts which are relevant for "memory" and lend themselves to observation and experimentation?

1. MEMORY AND CONSERVATION OF THE PAST

A person's past is at first ("first" in the developmental order) his entire heredity, and if we can consider heredity as a kind of phyletic memory, as much as conservation of "genetic information," we are, on this basis, extremely far from a particular act of recognition, or even more so of recall through memory-images. And nevertheless, conservation of hereditary past plays a role in all our actions, thus in each acquisition,[1] and, consequently, in each recognition or mnemonic recall, even if the content recognized or recalled is evidently acquired and not innate.

A first problem is thus to separate memory of acquisition, or memory in the proper sense of the word, from phyletic memory or conservation and use of inherited information. This separation is not as easy as it might seem. In the field of ethology, suppose an animal, sensitive to the "significant innate signs" (IRM—Internal Releasing Mechanisms— like the form or outline of twigs collected by a bird who builds his nest), recognizes them easier after several experiences, memory thus acquired would naturally be in part a function of the underlying hereditary mechanism. Even in human psychology it is very possible that memory for a perceptual figure of simple geometric character is facilitated, not by an IRM, but by certain functional mechanisms of spatial perception which require a part of innate influence. Similarly in this case memory or acquisition would not be (or not radically) separate from heredity.

[1] We know, in effect, that in contemporary biology every phenotypic acquisition presupposes an interaction, in various degrees, between the immediate environment and the synthetic activities of the gene and the germinating system.

But a second problem is even larger (in the case of humans) and even more important for us: in addition to hereditary schematism, there exist a considerable number of acquired schemes, perceptual schemes, schemes of habit or sensory-motor intelligence, conceptual preoperational schemes, operational schemes, etc., where conservation is totally dependent upon action unless conservation of the past necessarily depends on what we generally call memory. What are their connections with it?

The problem is not reduced to a question of vocabulary. But it comes up first, and it is convenient to begin by paying attention to the words we use. Biologists and psychologists do not always use the term memory in the same sense, and we can distinguish the three major meanings as follows:

I. Biologists speak of "memory" to designate the conservation of all acquired responses starting from the level of the facts of immunity. . . . In this first very broad meaning covering the conservation of any somatic acquisition as well as that of any schemes acquired from behavior, we will use the term "memory in the biologist's sense."

II. In a more restricted sense, reserved for the levels of a single behavior, we often speak of memory in as wide a fashion, which covers the conservation of habits or the results of learning as well as the recall of memory images or the facts of simple recognition. It is appropriate in this regard to pay attention to at least three points.

In the first place, it appears evident that the functioning of any habit presupposes recognition of certain signs: when Patelle[2] finds her place again on a certain rock after her displacement by the high tide, it is clear that she depends on certain proprio- and extero-ceptive cues and we thus have to admit that habit directs the responses of recognition. According to the vocabulary chosen, we could then say, either the habit is a particular case of memory, or habit is not a form of memory but enters into the recognitive memory. In both cases it is appropriate to distinguish two kinds of very different elements: on the one hand, conservation of sensory-motor schemes consisting of habit, and on the other hand, recognition of perceptual cues where meaning is determined by the schemes. In effect, whether we call everything memory or only recognition, it is one thing to reproduce an organized collection of movements (sensory-motor scheme) and another to recognize a perceptual cue.

In the second place, if we include in memory the conservation (and the possibility of repetition or of actualization) of each scheme of habit, there is no reason for not including in the same category of mechanisms

---

[2] *Translators' note.* Patelle is a cone-shaped mollusk.

conservation or actualization of all schemes of actions, knowledge or operations. The child thus learns to order or classify objects and the schemes are conserved, of such a kind that they are actualized in all situations where they are useful to the subject ...

In the third place, it is appropriate to distinguish carefully not only the repetition of a schematized act (from habit to operation) and the behaviors of recognition or recall, but also the two following forms of conservation of the past. On the one hand, this conservation could deal with processes susceptible of repetition, like a habit or an operation. But, on the other hand, this conservation of the past could also affect singular objects or events. We thus recognize a particular face among a hundred others and we can recall it by a strictly individualized memory image. This distinction of being repeatable and unique recovers in part that of the conservation of schemes and of memory of recognition or of recall, but the relationship remains to be specified. We learn, for example, a poem "by heart" by means of a series of repetitions, when it concerns a particular and individualized poem. Is it then a question of conservation of a scheme or of acts of recognition and recall? We answer: both. This maintains the distinction but poses the problem of relations. On the one hand, in effect, poetry, once learned, is susceptible of recall, but this recall, being complex, involves a learning and it comes back, ordinarily, to constructing a scheme and conserving it. On the other hand, beside more or less general schemes, one can have some individualized ones, just as in logical classification there can exist singular classes.[3]

To sum up, it is appropriate to focus our vocabulary on these points and begin to formulate our problems. The first of these two tasks, whether a purely semantic one, is important because a system of definitions could lead either to nothing in masking the problems or to explaining them. We will not call memory only the conservation of an earlier behavior and we will use the terms "schematism" or "conservation of schemes" to mean the capacity of subjects to reproduce that which is generalizable in a system of actions or of operations (scheme of habit of any kind: sensory-motor, conceptual, operational schemes, etc.); and we shall call "memory in the wider sense" what includes among other things this "conservation of schemes." We could be tempted to answer that the existence or construction of a scheme is one thing (for example of seriation or classification) and another thing is its conservation, which presupposes a sort of specialized memory. But the property of a scheme (as opposed to a behavior executed once) is precisely to connect one to others of analogous situations. ...

[3]Only individualized schemes are always part of a general system: the exception which they might seem to constitute is therefore only apparent.

III. We shall call on the other hand "memory in the strict sense" the responses related to recognitions (in the presence of the object) or to recall (in its absence) and of which the first distinct criterion is explicit reference to the past: the subject recognizes an object or a sequence of events if he has the impression of having already seen them (rightly or wrongly, for there are false remembrances); and the memory image in the mnemonic recall is generally different from the representative image (reproductive or anticipatory) in the fact that it is accompanied by a localization in the past (global or detailed, correct or incorrect) manifesting itself by the impression of having been experienced or perceived at some particular moment in the past (even though the time is not specified) and not only of that which is known in general and even less that which is foreseen. This first criterion goes with a second indicated immediately and perhaps more important even though it cannot be disassociated from the preceding one: memory in the strict sense and the memory image bear only on situations, processes or objects, which are unique and recognized or recalled as such, in contrast to schemes, which are general (the scheme of seriation or the concept of squareness, etc.) or to representative images which, however individual, symbolize a general scheme (the image of a square as symbol of all squares). . . . the possibility of intermediaries between memory and conservation of a scheme. . . .

The first difference between memory thus defined[4] and conservation of schemes is, then, that the latter are actualized in the present situation without explicit reference to the past, except if this new usage is

[4]We often distinguish, in addition to recognition and recall, a third form of memory related to the acceleration of acquisition in relearning. We observe, indeed, that when the result of learning is apparently erased, relearning gives the same results as before (or better) but with a saving in time or number of necessary trials: from which the hypothesis of retained "traces" between the two, thus of a memory whose manifestations would then be different from those of recognition or of recall.

But we have to agree when we introduce a necessary distinction between what the subject is able to "do," and the recognitions or recall which eventually accompany his actions, if it is only a question of reproduction of acts, we do not leave the domain of sensory-motor schemes (habits, etc.), and the observed ease in relearning shows simply that the initially constructed scheme from the first learning is not completely annihilated but is partly conserved. If on the other hand, relearning is accompanied by recognitions (of dispositioned or executed acts) and a fortiori of recall (memory images of previous sessions) then, indeed, there is "memory in the strict sense," being added to conservation of schemes, and that anew because there is explicit reference to the past.

In other words, if there is not reproduction facilitated by previous actions, the reference to the past does not exist in the subject's mind, but only in the experimenter's, and we speak then only of schematism or conservation of schemes. If, on the other hand, reference to the past exists from the subject's point of view and not simply from the observer's, then, and only then, we would use the term "memory in the strict sense".
. . .

accompanied by memories (mnesics), which could perhaps sometimes be useful but never necessary. A habit could thus be exercised without any memory of its formation; a scheme of seriation or of correspondence could also be applied without a recall of the past, etc. From the point of view of development, it is to be noted that a whole sensory-motor schematism is formed during the first 12 to 18 months of existence, where memory of recall was formed without depending on semiotic function. On the other hand, the application of these schemes presupposes a certain recognition (analogy of situations, etc.) and even the functioning of an elementary habit implies, as already stated, a recognition of cues. In a general way, assimilation which engenders a scheme is always reproductive at the same time, generalizable and recognitive in the sense that it contains factors of repetition, extension and discrimination, which marks a very primitive connection between schematism and recognitive memory (which presents a considerable advancement in comparison to recall). But the problem is to interpret the nature of this connection. One could in this regard at first distinguish two extreme types of recognition.

One is of clearly mnemonic character and appears when there is a new perception of the same individual object: at a certain level the infant recognizes his mother and distinguishes her from a stranger. But the other type has a kind of prenotional character and is in any case clearly schematic: it is the assimilation of a situation to a scheme, as when the baby, in the presence of a new object, suspended where others were previously seen, recognizes in it an object to swing. It is in this second sense that assimilation is always recognitive at the same time as reproductive and creative. The question is then to establish if mnemonic recognition is derived from recognitive assimilation, or the reverse, or if they are always connected. But even so, mnemonic recognition would constitute only a particular aspect of schematism in its totality and that would never explain the conservation of schemes through memory in the strict sense.

On the other hand, if one of the fundamental differences between schematism and memory in the strict sense is, as we have seen, that the first always includes the general or repeatable, while the second, like perception itself, applies in a general way only to unique objects or events and appears to evoke these schemes, operations, or ideas only by way of concrete figuration (or even, as we shall see, by partly deductive reconstruction and more or less connected to language), a central problem presents itself to us in this connection. We will have to determine how much memory requires a reconstruction, as P. Janet thought when he connected it to "recitation behavior," and to what degree it subsists, between the registering of facts and their recall, by memory of unconscious pictures being conserved (such as those Penfield brings back with electrical stimulation of the temporal lobes.) Now, it is possible: (1) That memories depend on "unconscious" traces (to the extent that they exist without reaching that integration as Freud & Bergson claim) and that they are essentially of a concrete and imaginary kind; (2) That they are in some way themselves connected to the schematism of actions (with the possibility of affective schemes)[5]; and (3) That memory appears to recall more abstract realities (causal sequences, conceptual or operational realities), only to the degree that it also depends on a deductive or verbal reconstruction by being inserted more deeply into the system of schemes. But all this is still only hypothesis and the facts will permit us to say more possibly in the future.

In a general way, the differences between schematism and memory seem to depend essentially upon the fact that the first translates internal organization and the dynamism of behavior, an organization of which conservation is the expression of its very activity, whereas the second is either a figurative reading or a reconstruction of the results of this activity without succeeding or bearing on it. But, to clarify hypotheses which follow, we must first make an important statement, without which they might appear either senseless or completely commonplace.

Learning theorists usually claim that all mental development, including schemes, is due to learning, and memory is nothing more than the conservation of what has been learned, including of course the schemes themselves. In this case, our principal hypothesis would distinguish only in the heart of memory the image or symbolic elements and motor elements, which goes without saying. But in the perspective of our former and present works,[6&7] on learning, this does not account for the development, for, deep in the continued activities of the subject, we must distinguish, in addition to what he "learns" continuously from the external environment, those factors of self regulation and equilibration, in a word, of organization, which rather direct learning than result from it. Similarly, any organism submits itself to the environment only as functioning of internal processes of organization, in certain indissociable interactions, which exclude the hypothesis of purely exogenous acquisitions. In this perspective, the schemes, however continuously modified by learning (accommodations, but relating also to

[5]See Piaget, *La formation du symbole chez l'enfant,* Second edition, Delachaux and Niestle, Neuchâtel, 1959.
[6]See Vols. VII to X of "Études d'épistémologie génétique": *Apprentissage et connaissance, logique, apprentissage et probabilité, etc.*
[7]Research of B. Inhelder, M. Bovet, H. Sinclair, etc.

a constant assimilation), depend more on processes of development in general than on those of learning alone, and that is why the problem of conservation of schemes constitutes a wholly different question from that of memory in the strict sense.

In one brief word, the hypothesis from which we proceed makes sense only in the framework of a general theory of development, distinct from particular theories of learning, and that's why it might be useful now to look for the place of memory among the totality of cognitive functions.

2. THE PLACE OF MEMORY IN THE SYSTEM OF COGNITIVE FUNCTIONS

An organism is a machine which brings about transformations and indeed two kinds of transformations: on the one hand, it assimilates the environment while undergoing its constraints; that is, it constructs and conserves those forms of organization susceptible of maintaining exchange with the outside; on the other hand, it modifies the environment by those responses and above all by its behavior in the forms which appear at the same time as a prolongation and specialization of these two kinds of jointly responsible transformations, so that one could make the diagram shown as Fig. 1.

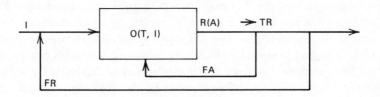

Figure 1

I = Input: O = Organization (system of internal transformations); R(A) = output or responses leading to TR = transformations of reality; FR = feedbacks from the results of TR; FA = feedback from the very actions which transform reality.

I. The inputs to the system (I) are the perceptions, but that does not mean that they constitute the only source of knowledge, even on the level of experience with objects. To know an object, it could operate on him, where the feedbacks FR carry back the results of his actions R, that means the TR, to the inputs I.

The interior of the system is not simply a collection of associative bonds connecting inputs I with responses R, but consists of an organization O which adds multiple elements to what is furnished at I. Cognitive organization is thus both assimilation of I data and transformation thereof. But internal transformations TI which constitute schematism at all levels, from elementary habits to high-level operations, depend only in part on the innate dispositions of the subject (spontaneous movements, reflexes, hereditary cerebral functioning, etc.) and are otherwise also being formed little by little under the increasing influence of the actions themselves R(A) which lead to transformations of reality TR; from there the feedbacks FA carry back from these actions R(A) to the internal organization O and this is what builds the schemes.

As to the outputs R, the diagram shows their outcomes under the name of transformation of reality TR and not of objects alone, for they could concern the body itself equally and include imitation or accommodation of the body depending on the properties of the object.

Thus diagramed, the cognitive functions make way for two important distinctions which we find useful for placing memory into such a picture. The first is that which confronts figurative and operative functions. These latter which extend from elementary actions all the way to higher functioning are characterized by their ability to transform the object. This does not mean, and we have constantly insisted in other writings, that logico-mathematical structures are drawn from the object as such; on the contrary they are abstracted by reflexive and constructive abstraction, from actions practiced upon the object and not from its properties. This is why the feedbacks FA connect the actions themselves in R to the internal organization O (whence the relative independence of the system of schemes). Figurative functions, on the contrary, do not tend to transform the object, but provide imitation in the largest sense of the word. Figurative instruments influence essentially the states, of which the configurations are the easiest to translate into images, and when they influence movements or transformations, it is then to present configurations without adding themselves to the modification. Such is at first perception (in I) which, even when directed by the action schemes of assimilation (whence a partial isomorphism between perception and intelligence), is essentially accommodation to the object, up to the point where perceptual activities imitate somewhat the form of the object (for example, when ocular movements follow contours). Such is also imitation (in I $\longrightarrow$ TR), which as early as the sensory-motor level furnishes a kind of image in acts of corporal models furnished on the other hand and even often by objects, and whose role we know in the future representation of the body itself. Imitation, at first immediate and external, later takes "different" and interiorized forms, from which a new fundamental figurative instrument for the construction of recall and which is the mental image, starting from interiorized imitation as we have tried to show elsewhere.[8] Likewise, symbolic play, the graphic image, etc., constitute or use figurative instruments born of imitation.

The formation of figurative functions is thus essentially connected to the feedbacks FR returning from the outcome of imitative actions in R to perceptions in I, whereas operational functions correspond at the same time to actions transforming the object in R $\longrightarrow$ TR and to internal operations in 0(TI), connected to each other by the feedback loop FA. But this is not to assume that there is no figural aspect in the interior organization 0(TI); since imitation is produced among others (in I), and perception insures inputs in I, we can presume that every scheme operating in 0(TI) carries at least some figural aspect, not because of the constituent or motor element, for the image is not an element of thought at all (which it would be if the internal system were not a transformational organization 0(TI), but a simple collection of transmissions by associative bonds) but because the cues or the symbols allow recognitions (from recognitive assimilation to perceptual recognition) and recall.

II. This leads us to the second major distinction that has to be introduced to cover the totality of cognitive functions: those of *signifier* and *signified*.[9] Understanding and intervention at R serve to manipulate objects, but give them meanings because they are assimilated beforehand to the organization at O. Then, meanings contain things signified which are the schemes which at all levels constitute the schematism of 0(TI) and also the things signifying. We have to distinguish three kinds of signifiers, of which the first two were provided by the instruments of the figurative functions and the third are collective and pose a problem of their own.

The most elementary signifiers (first developmentally) are nothing more than perceptual cues as Piéron[10] has judiciously held, preceded by the way by the great physicist Ampere.[11] Sensation is only a symbol (in the sense of a general signifier) and not a faithful copy of the object (it is why we speak here of imitation in the broad sense). A cue is only part of the object (a branch across a wall, cue to the presence of a tree),

[8]Piaget and Inhelder, *L'image mentale chez l'enfant,* Presses Universitaires de France, 1966.

[9]We call "signified" the meaning itself, this is the scheme or concept (in understanding) and not only the objects (in extension) to which they apply.

[10]H. Piéron, *La sensation, guide de vie* (Gallimard), pp. 412–413.

[11]See Barthelemy-Saint-Hilaire, *La philosophie des deux Amperes,* Second ed. (Didier), 1866, p. 34.

or one of these aspects (reflection, cue for a hardly visible surface of water) or again a causal result (an animal trace, stain, etc.): it is thus appropriate to serve as signifier for each sensory-motor scheme and when we say that any perception is meaningful, that means only that the signifier consists of perceptual cues, whereas what is signified is furnished by the schemes going beyond the sensory data (identifications, putting into relationships, etc., inherent in sensor-motor schemes or schemes of action, like conceptual schemes).

The second level of signifiers is formed during the second year and marks their differentiation in relation to things signified: these differentiating signifiers are no more simple parts or aspects of the perceived object but enter in when we have more or less similar or incited recall obtained in its absence; to say it another way, it is first symbols (in the strict linguistic sense, as opposed to "signs"), and these symbols are nothing more than figural instruments which have been dealt with before (except for perceptions themselves), thus images, symbolic games, etc. Now, as we have tried to show elsewhere,[12] it is imitation which, in surpassing its initial sensory-motor level to become differentiated and interiorized, is the source of differentiating signifiers which are figural as well as symbolic. To the use of such figural symbols corresponds the beginning of representation and we use the term "semiotic function" for the utilization of such symbols as well as the signs in question. Let us notice, moreover, with respect to organization of the operational schemes O(TI), that there is no reason to think that, if the sensory-motor schemes, as things signified, contain their signifiers in the form of perceptual cues, representative or operative schemes do not necessitate the use of adequate signifiers, they are constituted by the system of signs of language,[13] which we will return to later. But language is collective and does not meet all the individual needs: if it is adequate to designate general schemes, common to all individuals, it is not sufficient to signify the detail of experiences or the actions pursued by each particular individual and especially in what has to do with memory, which is what interests us here. Between perceptual cues and common language, imaged symbolism normally enters since the totality of signifiers corresponds to different and individual schemes.

The third level of signifiers then consists of language, or a system of different and collective "signs," arbitrary or conventional as well as collective. In order not to complicate the diagram, we have not distinguished in the subject's actions R $\longrightarrow$ TR individual and social actions for they are wholly indissociable. Now, any social group possesses a

[12]J. Piaget, *La formation du symbole chez l'enfant,* Delachaux and Niestle.
[13]Natural language or artificial systems of signs (algebra, etc.).

language, and, by its intervention, involves the cognitive internal organization of the individuals. We would have to complete the diagram used by introducing a third and fourth system of feedback loops F'A and F'R to represent the constant flashing back and forth on organization O(TI) and on inputs I, of collective actions at the center of which enter actions R $\longrightarrow$ TR of the individual subject, but since this is self-evident, it is useless to distinguish them from FA and FR. The only point to remember is the presence of linguistic signifiers, serving to signify the organizational schemes O(TI) in addition to imaged signifiers, for they play an important role in the functioning of memory.

Before returning to the latter of these, we see straight off that it is closely connected to figural aspects of knowledge and various systems of signifiers but let us sum up then, for clarification of what follows, the correspondences which exist between figural instruments of knowledge and semiotic function (symbols and signs). These are the areas of intersection (Fig. 2). First there are figural instruments not involved in the semiotic function: such as perception, which constitutes a system of signifiers, from the non-differentiated cues in the perceptual data. Then there are the mechanisms which are both figural and semiotic: such as the mental image, symbolic play, differentiated imitation, gestures, etc. Finally there is a category of semiotic instruments which are not themselves figural: the system of signs. Natural languages belong in this category. However, the usage the subject makes of this system is not necessarily devoid of a figural aspect. In particular, the use the child makes of language often recalls the use of a totality of symbols more than that of a system of signs. Even at the adult level, language whose signs are conventional or "arbitrary," are often close to figural expression: besides onomatopoeia, there is the whole play of metaphors and the expressiveness appropriate to "affective language" ... But even in this semantic kind of case the role of the structures of signs as signifiers is subordinated to the collective linguistic rules and uses, and the laws of signs are not reducible to those of the mental image or symbols available to individual construction. On the contrary, we have just seen, according to the developmental level (from 2 years), language

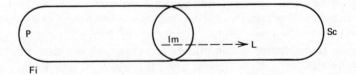

Figure 2

Fi = figural instruments; Se = semiotic function; P = perception;
Im = mental image, etc.; L = language.

varies somewhat in this respect: closer to the figural (and especially imitation) in early stages, it becomes progressively more remote in those that follow; whence the dotted arrow marks in Fig. 2, and simply reminds us of a genetic problem.

III. Such is, in three main lines, the system of cognitive functions other than memory itself (in the strict sense defined in III, section 1, p. 93) and we still have to find out where to locate it. But it is here that the problems which are not yet resolved begin, and in order to present evidence we started from these diagrams (Figs. 1 and 2). . . .

The central problem of memory lies in radical heterogeneity, from the point of view of the researcher (by way of the subject), of experimental observables and what goes on in the "black box," as embellished in the diagram of Fig. 1 of a transformational organization O(TI). The observables are located on the diagram as inputs I and outputs R $\longrightarrow$ TR and we speak of them by way of preamble: they are thus relative to what the subject knows (as earlier perceived) and to what he will recall. As to the hidden mechanisms in O(TI), they are the ones that guarantee conservation or construction of memory, and it is of these that we know nothing, at least in the case of recall.

In what concerns the observables, which we just mentioned, it seems clear that memory is tied very closely to figural and semiotic functions, and for two complementary reasons.

The first is that recognition and recall both depend upon figural or semiotic mechanisms. Recognition, which is a very primitive process existing even in lower invertebrates, is brought about in the presence of the perceived objects and consists in perception of something already known, that is as having been perceived before, which is a double use of the figural mechanism, perception. Whereas recall is possible only by means of a memory image, i.e., an image, or a "recitation," thus of language, which means of mechanisms both figural and semiotic (images) or purely semiotic (but if the word is not itself figural, the memory, or acoustic image of the word, is already figural).

The second reason is that reciprocally all semiotic mechanisms, if they are figural (image, symbolic play, etc.) or not (language), depend on memory. A mental image is always, in part, even if it has as function only the actual representation of a state (in the course, for example, of reasoning about transformations), a memory image, since the image is constructed and reappears only in the absence of the object of perception. The only valid distinction between any reproductive image and a memory image is that the latter refers explicitly to a particular object or event located by the subject in his past, but any image remains always implicitly connected with perceptions, also past, that it tries to imitate or copy and thus it also presumes recall.[14] Language, also, naturally requires memory for words, etc., and there are numerous cases of aphasia without intellectual difficulties demonstrating that if the loss of memory hinders language, it does not change the operative schemes. In other cases, equally interesting to us, language difficulties are accompanied by figural deficiencies (spatial representations) without operational disturbance in the situations where reasoning produces transformations requiring only little representation of non-perceptual states.

3. PROBLEMS TO BE STUDIED

This tight solidarity of memory and figural or semiotic mechanisms raises then the central problem of conservation of memory, thus of the "traces" necessary for recognition or recall, that is the non-observable memorial properties, situated within the black box [O(TI)] of Fig. 1.: The formulation of the problem brings us around then to examine the different types of conservation of the past, already touched on in section 1.

I. The fundamental fact in this regard is the difference (difference whether of kind or degree is what we must establish) between conservation of an operative scheme (actions or operations) and memorial conservation, connected as we have seen to the figurative or semiotic elements.

Conservation or memory of a word is something other than the word itself, for nothing requires the word to remain in memory (we see this in learning a foreign language); that is to say that in the word there does not exist any automatic functioning (doubtless not at the collective scale of linguistic restraints),[15] which forces it to be conserved in the individual's memory. Similarly, memory of an image is something other than the image itself, for nothing leads it to be preserved through its own functioning. It is true that an image is already a memory image since it refers to earlier perceptions, but that remembrance could be lost, and as an interiorized imitation, the image does not contain spontaneous self-preservation.

On the contrary, the property of a scheme is to maintain by its own functioning and to be preserved in the psychological sense by conservation of the past, for its own method of composition involves logical conservation, that is the invariance of the whole system across the transformations which it takes on. The property of an operative

---

[14]It retains anticipatory images, but they proceed by analogy with earlier experiences.
[15]Here is another vast problem for study.

scheme, for example, is to require a reversible structure, that is in nontemporal reality ... and assures conservation of the system by its internal logic which requires the interdependence of its constituents. As a result memory of an operative scheme like classification, seriation or biunivocal correspondence (we even say memory of the scheme as opposed to that of concrete objects which could be seriated or classified, etc.) is mistaken for the scheme itself, which, once constructed, is conserved throughout life except for pathological accidents. It is there, in fact, something wholly other than memory in the strict sense. A gestaltist answered us once that that was entirely true, and that memory of a *Gestalt,* for example, is nothing other than the *Gestalt* itself. I agree, if we recognize that the *Gestalt* is already a scheme (generalizable, etc., by its symmetry, regularity, etc.) but one can also say the same for a perception; besides, a "bad" form or irregular *Gestalt* is not precisely conserved as such in the remembrance and its memory is equally something other than perceptual registering.

At the other extreme of the different kinds of schematisms, remember that a vital organization also is conserved by virtue of its functioning and that an organism continues to live, at least in its immortal parts like the genome, without the existence of a particular function of conservation or of memory of the organization. We would say that this function exists and that its name is heredity. But, because the genome is a regulatory system (and not as we once believed an atomistic collection of genes independent one of the others), we have to distinguish precisely between heredity, which is a transmission of particular characteristics through divisions and multiplications, and the organization as such which is not properly speaking transmitted, but continues and is presented as the necessary condition for any transmission.[16]

To return to psychology and schematism acquired or "constructed" in the course of development and not innate or organic, the opposition between memory in the strict sense and the conservation of schemes in their higher or operational form is surely lessened as soon as we go down to the elementary levels, such as those of sensory-motor schemes, and in particular to schemes of habit. Indeed, a habit can be lost and its conservation is thus tied to certain conditions of functioning. We should then examine this situation of the schemes at lower levels and pose the problem of the possibility of non-existence of series of intermediaries between memorial conservation and conservation of schemes.

Let us state at first that the schemes appropriate to sensory-motor intelligence are still closely related, as far as their self-preservation

[16]See Piaget, *Biologie et connaissance* (Gallimard, 1967), Chap. VII.

through functional regulations is concerned, to that which we observe at the time of operative schemes. Some schemes such as those of permanence of an object after perceptual disappearance, or the practical organization of displacement in a "group" in the geometric sense of the term, are conserved throughout life because they are prolonged afterwards in operative structures. Similarly, if some particular schemes such as drawing to oneself an object by means of certain intermediaries (supports, strings, stick) in order to swing a suspended object, etc., are not indefinitely generalizable, their general coordinations (nesting of schemes, order of succession, correspondences, etc.) point on the contrary to a sufficiently permanent schematism, so permanent even that we have to look there for the elementary source of logical operations. We have to envisage the possibility of different degrees of generality, but, from the very start, we can assume the presence of auto conservation indispensable for the functioning of intelligence (all as the result, typically, of a progressive construction).

In what concerns the schemes of the most primitive habits, certain ones are lost in the normal individual, like sucking the thumb; others are conserved throughout life like those related to visual or tactile-kinesthetic exploration. The question then centers on the conditions of the mechanism of conservation or extinction and we see straightaway that this conservation is due to feedbacks maintaining the scheme as a function of its use and of its results. Isn't it then exactly the same with remembrances belonging to memory in the strict sense, which are strengthened when they are used frequently and favorably or extinguished for lack of usage or also because they are suppressed when disagreeable? Perhaps, but with two cautions, which are essential and which force us to see this eventual assimilation as a problem and not as a given fact from which to start.

In the first place, a habit (and this is true *a fortiori* of all schematisms of higher ranks than this) is a system of groups which functions as a totality, and it is precisely this functioning of the group which insures the conservation of the system, however elementary it may be; this system is also closed on itself and thus constitutes a scheme (it is all the more self-evident if the scheme represents a subsystem of a larger one that includes it, like Hull's "habit family hierarchy"). A remembrance, on the other hand, could either appear isolated (sudden reappearance of a melody or a neighbor's face as he steps from an airplane), or it forms part of a system (and this could be the case even of isolated remembrances), but nothing proves that the system is of purely memorial nature (in the strict sense) and everything seems to indicate on the contrary that it includes an important part of action and consequently a more or less extensive schematism. In this case, the question is to know if conservation belonging to memory in the strict sense is independent of that of schemes or if it depends on it more or less directly and how. For, we know that there exist some properly memorial schemes, studied by F. Bartlett, and some of which constitute spontaneous memory-technical processes, but we still have to establish their relations with cognitive schemes and to conduct this study on the genetic level or within general mental development. Furthermore, we best remember and maintain the distinction between the "schema" belonging to images and the action "scheme," the first resulting in simplification and the second in assimilations by way of analogies.

In the second place, there is a large category of mnemonic processes of which the elementary kinds are manifestations connected to a conservation of action schemes: there are facts of recognition which, in their initial forms, are solidary with sensory-motor schemes. In effect, all habits presuppose recognitions of cues and successive phases of a practical act of intelligence are equally determined by the successive cues for which recognition is indispensible to the performing of the action. In this case, one could reasonably suppose that memorial conservation is subordinate to that of schemes, which is the same as saying that mnemonic recognition stems from recognitive assimilation. In higher forms of recognition on the other hand, one can perhaps recognize an object seen only once in the past and seemingly independent of any schematism. But we still have to examine if this *hapax* does not constitute a special class in the total classification, or, to state it otherwise, if recognition is not then solidary with a complex system and not conscious of analogies and oppositions which would explain why the isolated object has sufficiently caught our attention, at the time of the first perception, in order to be recognized the second time.

Finally, as far as memory of recall is concerned, the problem of memorial conservation remains most delicate. Between the opinions of authors, like Freud and Bergson, who believe that all the past is registered, and remains in the unconscious (but they do not tell us how, as if the mere fact of later recall was enough to explain the supposed conservation between the fixation of the remembrance and its reappearance) and the theories like Janet's which admit that every recall is a reconstitution without other intermediary traces, since the fixation, that the facts, material and exterior evidence, permit this reconstitution, there is room for all these hypotheses.

Among others this is the problem which we have to study, but, if we dare to approach it, it is because up to now the possible conservation of the remembrance has been too little compared with the evident conservation of the operative schemes, just as we have analyzed too little the memorial reconstruction in Janet's sense ("recitation behavior") in its relations with deductive or operative reconstructions. A perspective too much neglected perhaps in the studies of memorial processes is that of comparative and functional analysis of the collection of cognitive mechanisms beginning with intelligence in its multiple manifestations: it is from such a point of view that we must examine certain aspects of the development of memory.

II. Classical studies of memory remained astonishingly positivistic, that is to say, limited to inputs to and outputs from the black box (I and R in our Fig. 1), in varying with great ingenuity different factors of the stimulus, but without going beyond the observables to look for what makes up the interior of the black box. Ebbinghaus wanted to stay with the psycho-physical methods for analyzing the laws of memory and, since then, an impressive collection of quantitative data has been accumulated in this narrowly defined area.

But if one is interested in the contents of the box which has remained too well closed (by methodology perhaps more than by pressure), it is certainly appropriate to limit one's ambitions, but also to look for ways to justify them. To limit them is easy: we shall look only for qualitative analysis, not attempting to discover new laws of memory, but to look for mechanisms connecting those of image and intelligence. The justification for such a project could be rooted in two kinds of considerations. One is that the internal unfolding of the intellectual process is scarcely more accessible than in the case of memory ("thought is an unconcious activity of the mind," Binet said at the end of a study of provoked introspection): the analysis of intellectual behaviors, that is responses of subjects in conflict with problems, suffices meanwhile to allow certain reconstitutions, whose validity is more or less controllable by examination of the implications which they contain. Why then not try an analogous venture in the domain of memory?

In the second place, the difficulties of the problem of mnemonic recall are not insurmountable unless we worked with adults, whose mental functions have reached too complex and too crystallized a state of achievement to understand the intimate processes. To use on the other hand once more the genetic method one could reckon on attaining, in response to questions of memory, more than successes in percentages of subjects or in fractions of the total task: one could hope to obtain the qualitatively distinct stages furnishing some glimmers about the organization of memory.

But, to come closer to such a goal, we naturally have to choose factors and make them vary as function not so much with quantitative care (number of presentations, temporal intervals between them, etc.), but with the general problem. Thus, our central question is the comparison of memory in the strict sense and the conservation of preoperational and operational schemes. We have thus begun our research on memory,[17] by studying the remembrance of an operative situation, either an hour after presentation of the display, or after one or two weeks, or even in several cases after an interval of four to eight months. The apparatus consists, for example, in purely static states, but results from an operative transformation (which is not indicated to the child), such as ten little sticks arranged in order of size or collections of classifiable objects, or even two lines of equal length, one straight and the other bent. Or else we present the child with a series of transformations such as pourings from one vessel into another which show certain relations of transitivity or associativity of equivalences. Since the operational level of the child was known in other ways, one could first have wondered if the remembrance of the apparatus consisted of a passive or receptive registering of what he had perceived (in the sense of perception as such and not of interpretation) or if the child would recall only what he understood. Now except in several very young subjects, memory is found very closely adjusted to understanding. This result, banal at first, is nevertheless interesting to analyze closely, for it is amazing to see not only how recall after a week or two correlates with the detail of operational and preoperational stages and substages well known to us, but also how much, at these levels, remembrance is connected to what the child knows how "to do," that is to what he knows how to construct effectively. But the big surprise which the data have revealed to us is that, in a certain case, like the perception of a sequence of seriated elements, after six months memory is found at a higher level than after one week, without any new presentation of the apparatus. It goes without saying that such facts remind us of Ballard's "reminiscences" phenomenon and are instructive from the point of view of conservation or of memorial reconstruction.

But such progress is not general and is naturally connected to the nature of the scheme on which the recall applies or to which is attached in one way or another, the memory.... We shall see that if memory is not connected to a dominant scheme (like seriation) but to two long uncoordinated schemes (numerical correspondence acquired at about 7 years and conservation of length at only about 9 years), the conflict which results tends to deteriorate the memory, which is then oriented toward illusory solutions for lack of sufficient operative support. It was therefore appropriate to vary the apparatus presented, according to a

[17]Which was tackled already elsewhere in connection with the mental image in a chapter on the qualities of the image after simple perception of the model or after action of material reproduction.

gradation leading from the more to the less operative. Certain apparatuses have been chosen which can contain either an operative interpretation, or a predominately figural impression: a rotation of a triangle with figural cues differentiating the apexes, pictures of a bottle tipped or lying down with colored liquid filling part of it, a snail in different positions on the rim of a horizontal figure eight (∞) or two bent tubes each containing liquid with equal levels in both branches of one and unequal levels in the other (one then closed with a cork). Finally other apparatuses are constructed of geometrical figures with bars in relatively contingent positions, memory then having to depend on only a minimum of operative schemes.

Briefly, the problem is to free the possible relations between memory and the operational or preoperational schematism, and it was suitable to foresee some more or less schematizable or more or less figural presentations. But it is especially advisable, to notice that if, in broad outline, schemes mean general aspects of actions or operations, whereas memory images belong to concrete or unique objects or configurations, there is still a great variability in this connection. Besides very general schemes which correspond to logical operations of the most constant use, it is necessary to foresee the existence of schemes more and more specialized and in more possible ways. At the operational level, there may be specialization of schemes according to whether one passes from a system to a subsystem (rotations as subgroups of displacements, etc.) and especially according to the numerous distinct cases of application of the same scheme (seriation of lengths or of areas, weights, etc.) At the preoperational level, schemes are more and more special if one passes from articulated intuitions through regulations to the simplest intuitions connecting such or such more or less isolatable action and especially if one passes from more or less general schemes of habits to schemes of momentarily repeatable but not indefinitely durable actions.

The simplest hypothesis as to the correspondence between memory in the strict sense and schematism is then that the first consists only of translation of the figural aspects of the second. Recognition starts from a connection with perceptual cues belonging to sensory-motor schemes, and we can only assume that, at all levels, recognition is also connected to more and more specialized schemes of assimilation. Recall could be understood as the product of a union between a certain reconstruction, inferential in various degrees, and the use of "traces" susceptible of unconscious conservation. Now, representation definitely presupposes the use of schemes available to the subject at the moment of recall, if only for reconstituting the temporal order of remembrance, which is doubtless not given in conservation itself. As to the latter, the "traces" or witness elements it uses or which constitute the maintenance of them could be connected with concrete and imagined representations of the specialized schemes, serving them with individual symbolism (and the resemblance to the symbol could be more or less exact), just as language designates the more general schemes. Thus conservation of what is remembered, doubtless always more or less fragmentary, would depend upon that of the schemes of habit and intelligence and would ordinarily be completed by a reconstruction using the actual schemes exercised.

III. Such being the general hypothesis by which we have been inspired in this work and which directed the experiments,[18] it is perhaps advisable to develop it a little bit, in order to make more understandable the interpretations of some facts which we will describe.

The common ground between conservation of schemes belonging to operative aspects of action or of intelligence and the figural elements of perception (recognition) or the memory images (recall) belonging to memory in the strict sense is to be found in the connections between schematizing assimilation and the various possible forms of accommodation of the same schemes to the objects assimilated, if these are present, as in the multiple actual cognitive adaptations, or belongs to the past as in memory.

Every scheme is the result of an assimilatory activity with the property of incorporating the new to the known or of reproducing and, sooner or later, of generalizing what has just been discovered: assimilation is thus necessary in forming schemes and they are only the structural result of its functioning in a circle comparable to that of judgment and concept (particular cases, on the plane of representation, of intelligent assimilation and of the scheme).

But every assimilatory scheme has to accommodate itself to the objects to which it is applied, otherwise assimilation could only be deforming (or centered on the affectivity of the self as in the case of symbolic play where reality is modified to meet the desires of the moment): perceptual-motor or representative accommodation, etc. Assimilation without accommodation does not exist, nor conversely accommodation without assimilation, which makes us understand the indissociable connection of recognition and memory images with schemes of assimilation.

It is indeed accommodation which is at the starting point of the figural aspects of knowledge. On the level of perception, perceptual

---

[18]To be truthful, and this is perhaps the last chance to confess it, we didn't count at first on studying only memory of operational situations. But the problems which we uncovered were extended irrevocably all the way to those we have just shown in the guise of an Introduction.

schemes are directed by assimilation in their general orientation of identification and comparison, but they are accommodators to the degree that there is exploration of the perceived configuration, following of the contours and the articulations of the figure, etc. Generally on the plane of action, accommodation remains in equilibrium (as at the perceptual level) with assimilation insofar as adaptation to new situations and intelligent understanding is concerned, but it could also tip the scales and be of interest in itself: it is oriented then in the direction of imitation (just as the primacy of assimilation leads to play, as remembered at the time). Imitation, already at work in the wide sense in perceptual exploration which follows the contours of the object, is specialized in a sensory-motor or particular sensory-tonic function, whose development leads, well before the construction of the semiotic function, to a sort of representation in material acts and better and better molds of exterior models. Then, it is this imitation which constitutes the source, once susceptible of functioning in a different and interiorized state, not only of the mental image itself, but doubtless of the semiotic function in general, as differentiation of signifiers and things signified.

On the other hand, as memory in the strict sense rests on the use of figural instruments, perceptual for recognition and imaged recall (as also imitative in the strict sense for "reconstructions" which we will have located between recognition and recall), it follows then that it depends essentially on an accommodation more or less differentiated and unique to the model to be recognized or rediscovered, and consequently of an assimilation to schemes since every accommodation is solidary with such an assimilation.

But a problem is then naturally posed, not otherwise specific to memory in general and which already enters in the case of imitation (that is in fact one particular form of memory of "reconstruction"): it is to establish, given the indefinite diversification of accommodations sources of memory images or recognitions, whether it is elaborated as much by schemes of assimilation as by the individualized varieties of accommodation. In effect schemes of accommodation do not exist (only "schemas"), since every scheme is the result of assimilations. On the other hand, these as well as the schemes constituting their results are oriented toward generality, whereas all accommodation, and in particular the memory-images which could result, are oriented toward the singular: it is to the same degree that accommodation is particularized that it becomes the source of figural instruments. But the property of schemes, precisely because of their characteristic of generality, is to contain nested hierarchies, the most general including the sub-schemes and after them up to unique schemes (that is of unique term) whose method of specific assimilation is identification. On the contrary, accommodation could be more or less advanced and exact, or remain global, but does not contain nesting. There is then no contradiction in seeing in memory in the strict sense the result of differentiated or individualized accommodations and to consider conservation of memories as necessarily solidary with that of schemes of assimilation; and this hypothesis is not reduced to a simple tautology consisting of identifying conservation and assimilation which would explain nothing, but that means to presuppose that conservation of an element (or individualized sub-scheme) is a function of that of more and more general schemes which it heralds, and even often of the system in its totality. Then, it is there that we try to show: that memories are connected, under various forms, to schemes of actions and operations whose influence remains constantly discernable in the subject's memory according to his operational level.

IV. The preliminary or even fundamental problem of memory tends then to be displaced from memory in the strict sense to memory in the wider sense, that is, to be centered on the conservation of the schematism itself, from individualized and figuratively accommodated schemes up to the most general schemes, for, even in our hypothesis, conservation of these latter finally would support all the weight of the mnemonic apparatus. Now we will speak of this central problem, and we have to say why.

There are two reasons. One is that, from the psychological point of view, this conservation is self-evident as we have seen under I, for the property of a generalizing assimilation is to function constantly in new ways, that is, to be conserved itself through its reproductive or generalizable activity, which assures the conservation of whatever scheme it becomes. The other is that if we ask how this continuity of functioning is assured, that is in the end this conservation in its more elementary and formatory aspect, one immediately has to leave the field of behavioral psychology, and fall back on the facts of neurophysiology, of biology in general and even to those of biochemistry.

To begin with psychology, schemes of assimilation could be of three kinds according to their method of conservation: preoperational schemes like habits (in the wide sense and as early as perceptual schemes), preoperational schemes evolving toward being reversible and schemes properly operational. The first are conserved by their own exercise (reproductive and generalizable assimilation) but they weaken in case of nonfunctioning. The second ones show the same but less stable type of conservation in the sense that they evolve in the direction of a final equilibrium (ready to be integrated into other schemes in the process), and that the phases of this equilibration are themselves only transitory. This means that each of these phases is not conserved indefinitely but that each tends toward the following, the conservation in question being therefore that of an organism or of an organ in the process of development. It is in such situations that we can observe a progression in memory every several months, as just reported in the case of seriation.

As to operational schemes in the narrow sense, that is, having arrived at the level of reversible operation, remember that their distinctive characteristic is the state of equilibrium, which expresses causally the character of reversibility. Now, when we say equilibrium, we say conservation. That is why schemes of seriation, of numeration (series of natural numbers), etc. are conserved during all of life once they are constructed, and that precisely because of their operational and equilibrated or reversible nature. The best verification at our disposal for controlling this conservation of operational schemes in the course of formation or as soon as they are constructed is furnished by the longitudinal research conducted by one of us on children of different ages questioned during 4 or 5 years on problems of conservation of quantities, etc. Now, during this lapse of time, no regression whatsoever could be observed from one stage or substage to a preceding one.

If we pass from simple psychological observations to the biological data capable of accounting for this conservation of schemes, there are two kinds which are equally important for us. The first are drawn from procedures leading to suppressing or weakening the effects of learning: electroshock or drugs (especially those which retard the formation of RNA) acting in a different or cumulative way. The principal lessons to be drawn concern the spontaneous consolidation of memories as well as the possible recovery of traces apparently lost.

Consolidation of "memories" is manifested in that the effects of suppression of the results of learning are much less strong as the application of the stated procedure is delayed. All this happens then as if after a phase of "short-term memory" in the course of which the traces are registered or organized, there is a phase of "long-term memory" marking their stabilization. When, on the other hand, the traces apparently lost are subsequently recovered, the process of recuperation could be accelerated or retarded by physical means, notably by those which facilitate or inhibit the formation of RNA.

The second important data refer to the role of RNA. Babich, Jacobsen, and Bubash have, for example, shown that if one injects into the nervous system (of untrained rats) some RNA from rats which have undergone preliminary learning (association of a sound with food), he finds they learn more rapidly. Not confirmed by Gross and Carey, this experiment has been successfully done again by Fjerdingstad, Nissen and Peterson. On the other hand and above all, Baron and Cohen (1966) have been able to establish, using actinomycin C or D (which curbs the action of messenger RNA) or puromycin (acting on the proteins themselves whose synthesis is due to DNA by the intervention of this RNA), the possibility of inhibiting, either short-term memory (immediately after learning), or long-term memory (that connected to the integration of the synthesis of the proteins whereas the first is to the modifications of the configuration of the proteins under the dependence of the RNA).

What interests us in such facts is thus that the registering of "traces" as early as the initial phase (short-term memory), and their conservation in the course of the second phase (long-term memory), seems to be one and the other dependent upon highly structured substances. The messenger RNA receives, in effect, information from DNA; that means that it is the carrier of hereditary schemes imprinting their structure on the proteins. If it is at the heart of such organization again so close to hereditary morphogenesis, and not in some neutral section (comparable to a *tabula rasa*) which could eventually offer the cytoplasm of the nerve cell, that brought about the registration and consolidation of memory "traces," it means that, at the biochemical level, memory would be subordinate to a structuration, thus to a schematism: in other words, new connections (introduced by learning would not constitute independent elements or annexations simply added to the hereditary schemes, but would seem straightway integrated because of new links in a chain resulting from activity of those schemes and presupposing accommodation of them to the situation imposed during learning. To say it differently, the collaboration necessary of RNA, insofar as it emanates from DNA, would show that traces could be integrated only at the heart of a previous organization (which here is directly dependent on the genes but could be at other levels dependent on them in a more and more indirect way) and this would be a fact comparable to what we believe we have found at all levels of behavior by saying that conservation of memory is subordinate to that of schemes or of structures which are greater in generality. It is true that this intervention of RNA may be interpreted in several ways. Before we conclude that it is for acquired memory what DNA is for hereditary memory, that is a carrier or a transmitter, we have to know (as McConnell himself says, the author of the much discussed experiments on Planaria at Michigan), whether RNA does not act simply as an instrument of generalized sensitization for the stimuli, which helps the conditioning. The fact that RNA plays an essential role in the synthesis of proteins makes us understand that it is integrally necessary for the building up of memory, but in what form? We shall therefore be satisfied to state that the orientation of the current research leads us farther away from the model of the "engrams" (which are isolated and simply imprinted) and orients itself toward the idea that the registration of memory depends on structures which go beyond them in organization and in synthesizing power.

V. Within the framework of this introduction, let us summarize in a few words the principal hypotheses which we shall try to verify in this work. Memory is an accumulation of information coded because of processes of perceptual and conceptual assimilation. But this information is in part related to the code used, according to its potential nature, for example, effective or simply redundant. Now the variations of memory in the course of development are not only a function of the smaller or larger facilities of encoding and decoding: *the code itself is susceptible of being modified,* and that is what happens in connection with the construction of the operative schematism of the subject. As a result we can observe with age different types of organization of remembrances according to the level of the code of a subject, and also according to the transformation of the code during retention itself (for example when there is progression in memory without new presentation). This also requires the distinction between two different problems in conservation of memory: on the one hand, that of memory retention leading to decoding and *retrieval,*[19] (recognition, reconstitution and recall) as function of a code of a determined level: that is the problem of memory in the strict sense; but, on the other hand that of conservation of the code itself through possible transformations, and here we deal with the more general problem of conservation of schemes in the course of development.

[19]Output of information and reencoding.

A HISTORY OF PSYCHOLOGY
IN AUTOBIOGRAPHY

Autobiography

An autobiography has scientific interest only if it succeeds in furnishing the elements of an explanation of the author's work.[1] In order to achieve that goal, I shall therefore limit myself essentially to the scientific aspects of my life.

Many persons doubtless are convinced that such a retrospective interpretation presents no objective value, and that it is to be suspected of partiality even more than an introspective report. I myself had originally subscribed to this view. But, on rereading some old documents dating from my years of adolescence, I was struck by two apparently contradictory facts which, when put together, offer some guaranty of objectivity. The first is that I had completely forgotten the contents of these rather crude, juvenile productions; the second is that, in spite of their immaturity they anticipated in a striking manner what I have been trying to do for about thirty years.

There is therefore probably some truth in the statement by Bergson that a philosophic mind is generally dominated by a single personal idea which he strives to express in many ways in the course of his life, without ever succeeding fully. Even if this autobiography should not

Jean Piaget, "Jean Piaget" (autobiographical sketch) pp. 237–256, in *A History of Psychology in Autobiography, Vol. IV,* E. G. Boring, *et al,* editors, copyright © 1952 Clark University Press.
[1]Submitted in French and translated by Donald MacQueen of Clark University.

convey to the readers a perfectly clear notion of what that single idea is, it will at least have helped the author to understand it better himself.

I. 1896–1914

I was born on August 9, 1896 at Neuchâtel, in Switzerland. My father who is still active, has devoted his writings mostly to medieval literature, and to a lesser extent, to the history of Neuchâtel. He is a man of painstaking and critical mind, who dislikes hastily improvised generalizations, and is not afraid of starting a fight when he finds historic truth twisted to fit respectable traditions. Among many other things he taught me the value of systematic work, even in small matters. My mother was very intelligent, energetic, and fundamentally a very kind person; her rather neurotic temperament, however, made our family life somewhat troublesome. One of the direct consequences of this situation was that I started to forego playing for serious work very early; this I obviously did as much to imitate my father as to take refuge in both a private and a non-fictitious world. Indeed, I have always detested any departure from reality, an attitude which I relate to the second important influential factor of my early life, viz., my mother's poor mental health; it was this disturbing factor which at the beginning of my studies in psychology made me intensely interested in questions of psychoanalysis and pathological psychology. Though this interest helped me to achieve independence and to widen my cultural background, I have never since felt any desire to involve myself deeper in that particular direction, always much preferring the study of normalcy and of the workings of the intellect to that of the tricks of the unconscious.

From seven to ten years of age I became successively interested in mechanics, in birds, in fossils of secondary and tertiary layers and in sea shells. Since I was not yet allowed to write with ink, I composed (in pencil) a little pamphlet to share with the world a great discovery: the "autovap," an automobile provided with a steam engine. But I quickly forgot this unusual combination of a wagon and a locomotive for the writing (this time in ink) of a book on "Our Birds," which, after my father's ironic remarks, I had to recognize, regretfully, as a mere compilation.

At the age of ten, as soon as I had entered "Latin School," I decided to be more serious. Having seen a partly albino sparrow in a public park, I sent a one-page article to a natural history journal of Neuchâtel. It published my lines and I was "launched"! I wrote then to the director of the Musée d'histoire naturelle and asked his permission to study his collections of birds, fossils and shells after hours. This director, Paul Godet, a very nice man, happened to be a great specialist on mollusks. He immediately invited me to assist him twice a week—as he said, like the "famulus" to Faust—helping him stick labels on his collections of land- and soft-water shells. For four years I worked for this conscientious and learned naturalist, in exchange for which he would give me at the end of each session a certain number of rare species for my own collection and, in particular, provide me with an exact classification of the samples that I had collected. These weekly meetings in the director's private office stimulated me so much that I spent all my free time collecting mollusks (there are one hundred and thirty species and hundreds of varieties in the environs of Neuchâtel); every Saturday afternoon I used to wait for my teacher a half hour ahead of time!

This early initiation to malacology had a great influence on me. When, in 1911, Mr. Godet died, I knew enough about this field to begin publishing without help (specialists in this branch are rare) a series of articles on the mollusks of Switzerland, of Savoy, of Brittany and even of Colombia. This afforded me some amusing experiences. Certain foreign "colleagues" wanted to meet me, but since I was only a schoolboy, I didn't dare to show myself and had to decline these flattering invitations. The director of the Muséum d'histoire naturelle of Geneva, Mr. Bedot, who was publishing several of my articles in the *Revue suisse de Zoologie* offered me a position as curator of his mollusk collection. (The Lamarck collection, among others, is in Geneva.) I had to reply that I had two more years to study for my baccalaureate degree, not yet being a college student. After another magazine editor had refused an article of mine because he had discovered the embarrassing truth about my age, I sent it to Mr. Bedot who with kindness and good humor responded: "It is the first time that I have even heard of a magazine director who judges the value of articles by the age of their authors. Can it be that he has no other criteria at his disposal?" Naturally, these various articles which I published at such a young age were far from being accomplished feats. It was only much later, in 1929, that I was able to achieve something more significant in this field.

These studies, premature as they were, were nevertheless of great value for my scientific development; moreover, they functioned if I may say so, as instruments of protection against the demon of philosophy. Thanks to them, I had the rare privilege of getting a glimpse of science and what it stands for, before undergoing the philosophical crises of adolescence. To have had early experience with these two kinds of problematic approaches constituted, I am certain, the hidden strength of my later psychological activity.

However, instead of quietly pursuing the career of a naturalist which seemed so normal and so easy for me after these fortunate circumstances, between the ages of fifteen and twenty I experienced a series of crises due both to family conditions and to the intellectual curiosity characteristic of that productive age. But, I repeat, all those crises I was able to overcome, thanks to the mental habits which I had acquired through early contact with the zoological science.

There was the problem of religion. When I was about fifteen, my mother, being a devout Protestant, insisted on my taking what is called at Neuchâtel "religious instruction," that is, a six weeks' course on the fundamentals of Christian doctrine. My father, on the other hand, did not attend church, and I quickly sensed that for him the current faith and an honest historical criticism were incompatible. Accordingly I followed my "religious instruction" with lively interest but, at the same time, in the spirit of free thinking. Two things struck me at that time: on the one hand, the difficulty of reconciling a number of dogmas with biology, and on the other, the fragility of the "five" proofs of the existence of God. We were taught five, and I even passed my examination in them! Though I would not even have dreamed of denying the existence of God, the fact that anyone should reason by such weak arguments (I recall only the proof by the finality of nature and the ontological proof) seemed to me all the more extraordinary since my pastor was an intelligent man, who himself dabbled in the natural sciences!

At that time I had the good luck to find in my father's library *La philosophie de la religion fondée sur la psychologie et l'histoire* by Auguste Sabatier. I devoured that book with immense delight. Dogmas reduced to the function of "symbols" necessarily inadequate, and above all the notion of an "evolution of dogmas"—there was a language which was much more understandable and satisfactory to my mind. And now a new passion took possession of me: philosophy.

From this a second crisis ensued. My godfather, Samuel Cornut, a Romansh man of letters invited me about that same period to spend a vacation with him at Lake Annecy. I still have a delightful memory of that visit: We walked and fished, I looked for mollusks and wrote a "malacology of Lake Annecy," which I published shortly afterward in the *Revue savoisienne.* But my godfather had a purpose. He found me too specialized and wanted to teach me philosophy. Between the gatherings of mollusks he would teach me the "creative evolution" of Bergson. (It was only afterwards that he sent me that work as a souvenir.) It was the first time that I heard philosophy discussed by anyone not a theologian; the shock was terrific, I must admit.

First of all, it was an emotional shock. I recall one evening of profound revelation. The identification of God with life itself was an idea that stirred me almost to ecstasy because it now enabled me to see in biology the explanation of all things and of the mind itself.

In the second place, it was an intellectual shock. The problem of knowing (properly called the epistemological problem) suddenly appeared to me in an entirely new perspective and as an absorbing topic of study. It made me decide to consecrate my life to the biological explanation of knowledge.

The reading of Bergson himself which I did only several months later (I have always preferred to reflect on a problem before reading on it) strengthened me in my decision but also disappointed me somewhat. Instead of finding science's last word therein, as my good godfather had led me to hope, I got the impression of an ingenious construction without an experimental basis: Between biology and the analysis of knowledge I needed something other than a philosophy. I believe it was at that moment that I discovered a need that could be satisfied only by psychology.

II. 1914–1918

It was during this period that the curious phenomenon to which I alluded in my introduction began to happen. Not being satisfied with reading a lot (this in addition to the study of mollusks and preparation for the baccalaureate degree which I received in 1915 at the age of eighteen), I began to write down my own ideas in numerous notebooks. Soon these efforts affected my health; I had to spend more than a year in the mountains filling my forced leisure time with writing a sort of philosophic novel which I was imprudent enough to publish in 1917. Now, in reading over these various writings which mark the crisis and the end of my adolescence—documents which I had completely forgotten till I reopened them for this autobiography—surprisingly I find in them one or two ideas which are still dear to me, and which have never ceased to guide me in my variegated endeavors. That is why, however unworthy such attempt may seem at first, I shall try to retrace these early notions.

I began by reading everything which came to my hands after my unfortunate contact with the philosophy of Bergson: some Kant, Spencer, Auguste Comte, Fouillée and Guyau, Lachelier, Boutroux, Lalande, Durkheim, Tarde, Le Dantec; and, in psychology, W. James, Th. Ribot and Janet. Also, during the last two years before the baccalaureate, we had lessons in psychology, in logic and in scientific methodology given by the logician, A. Reymond. But for lack of a laboratory and guidance (there was no experimental psychologist at Neuchâtel, even at the university) the only thing I could do was to theorize and write. I wrote even if it was only for myself, for I could not think without writing—but it had to be in a systematic fashion as if it were to be an article for publication.

I started with a rather crudely conceived essay pretentiously entitled "Sketch of a neo-pragmatism"; here I presented an idea which has since remained central for me, namely, that action itself admits of logic (this contrary to the anti-intellectualism of James and of Bergson) and that, therefore, logic stems from a sort of spontaneous organization of acts. But the link with biology was missing. A lesson by A. Reymond on realism and nominalism within the problem area of "universals" (with some reference to the role of concepts in present-day science) gave me a sudden insight. I had thought deeply on the problem of "species" in zoology and had adopted an entirely nominalistic point of view in this respect. The "species" has no reality in itself and is distinguished from the simple "varieties" merely by a greater stability. But this theoretical view, inspired by Lamarckism, bothered me somewhat in my empirical work (viz., classification of mollusks). The dispute of Durkheim and Tarde on reality or non-reality of society as an organized whole plunged me into a similar state of uncertainty without making me see, at first, its pertinence to the problem of the species. Aside from this the general problem of realism and of nominalism provided me with an over-all view: I suddenly understood that at all levels (viz., that of the living cell, organism, species, society, etc., but also with reference to states of conscience, to concepts, to logical principles, etc.) one finds the same problem of relationship between the parts and the whole; hence I was convinced that I had found the solution. There at last was the close union that I had dreamed of between biology and philosophy, there was an access to an epistemology which to me then seemed really scientific!

Thus I began to write down my system (people will wonder where I got the time, but I took it wherever I could, especially during boring lessons!). My solution was very simple: In all fields of life (organic, mental, social) there exist "totalities" qualitatively distinct from their parts and imposing on them an organization. Therefore there exist no isolated "elements"; elementary reality is necessarily dependent on a whole which pervades it. But the relationships between the whole and the part vary from one structure to another, for it is necessary to distinguish four actions which are always present: the action of the whole on itself (preservation), the action of all the parts (alteration or preservation), the actions of the parts on themselves (preservation) and the action of the parts on the whole (alteration or preservation). These four actions balance one another in a total structure; but there are then three possible forms of equilibrium: (1) predominance of the whole with alteration of the parts; (2) predominance of the parts with alteration of the whole; and (3) reciprocal preservation of the parts and of the whole. To this a final fundamental law is added: Only the last form of equilibrium (3) is "stable" or "good," while the other two, (1) and (2), are less stable; though tending toward stability, it will depend on the obstacles to be overcome how closely (1) and (2) may approach a stable status.

If I had known at that time (1913–1915) the work of Wertheimer and of Köhler, I would have become a Gestaltist, but having been acquainted only with French writings and not yet able to design experiments for the verification of these hypotheses, I was bound to limit myself to the construction of a system. I find the rereading of these old papers extremely interesting, inasmuch as they represent an anticipatory outline of my later research: It was already clear to me that the stable equilibrium of the whole and of the parts (third form) corresponded to states of conscience of a normative nature; logical necessity or moral obligation, as opposed to inferior forms of equilibrium which characterize the non-normative states of conscience, such as perception, etc., or organismic happenings.

After my baccalaureate, I took to the mountains for a rest. During that time I was formally registered in the Division of Science at the University of Neuchâtel, so that, soon after my return, I was able to graduate in the natural sciences and then to take my doctor's degree with a thesis on the mollusks of Valais (1918). Though I was all the while greatly interested in courses in zoology (Fuhrmann), embryology (Béraneck), geology (Argand), physical chemistry (Berthoud) and mathematics (group theory was particularly important for me with respect to the problem of the whole and the parts), I was very eager to move to a larger university with a psychology laboratory where I could hope to carry out experiments to verify my "system."

It was in this area of research where the mental habits acquired from contact with zoology were to serve me well. I never believed in a system without precise experimental control. What I wrote for myself during my years at the lycée I deemed unworthy of publication, because it remained mere theory; its real value seemed to me to be an incentive for later experiments, whose nature at that time, however, I could not surmise.

Nevertheless, during the year I spent in the mountains I was haunted by the desire to create, and I yielded to the temptation. Not to compromise myself on scientific grounds, however, I avoided the difficulty by writing—for the general public, and not for specialists— a kind of philosophic novel the last part of which contained my ideas (1917). My strategy proved to be correct: No one spoke of it except one or two indignant philosophers.[2]

III. 1918–1921

After having received the doctorate in the sciences, I left for Zurich (1918), with the aim of working in a psychology laboratory. I attended two laboratories, that of G. E. Lipps and that of Wreschner, and also Bleuler's psychiatric clinic. I felt at once that there lay my path and that, in utilizing for psychological experimentation the mental habits I had acquired in zoology, I would perhaps succeed in solving problems of structures-of-the-whole to which I had been led by my philosophical thinking. But to tell the truth, I felt somewhat lost at first. The experiments of Lipps and Wreschner seemed to me to have little bearing on fundamental problems. On the other hand, the discovery of psychoanalysis (I read Freud and the journal *Imago,* and listened occasionally to Pfister's and Jung's lectures) and the teachings of Bleuler made me sense the danger of solitary meditation; I decided then to forget my system lest I should fall a victim to "autism."

[2]Here are some quotations from that work entitled *Recherche* (1917). It was a question of elaborating a "positive theory of quality taking into account only relationships of equilibrium and disequilibrium among our qualities" (p. 150). "Now there can be no awareness of these qualities, hence these qualities can not exist, if there are no relationships among them, if they are not, consequently, blended into a total quality which contains them while keeping them distinct. For example, I would not be aware either of the whiteness of this paper or of the blackness of this ink if the two qualities were not combined in my consciousness into a certain unit, and if, in spite of this unity, they did not remain respectively one white and the other black. . . . In this originates the equilibrium between the qualities: there is equilibrium not only among the separate parts in that way (and that occurs only in material equilibriums) but among the parts on the one hand, and the whole on the other, as distinct from the whole resulting from these partial qualities. . . . (It is therefore necessary to proceed from the whole to the parts and not from the part to the whole as does a physicist's mind)" (pp. 151–153). "One can then distinguish a first type of equilibrium where the whole and the part mutually sustain each other" (p. 156), and other types such that there be coordinated interaction between the whole and the parts (p. 157). Now "all equilibriums tend toward an equilibrium of the first type" (p. 157), but without being able to reach it on the organic level: "Therefore we call an ideal equilibrium the equilibrium of the first type and real equilibrium that of the other types, although every real equilibrium, whatever it be, presupposes an ideal equilibrium (p. 158). In contrast, the first type is realized on the level of thought: It is "the origin of the principle of identity, from which the principle of contradiction is deduced," etc. (p. 163).

In the spring of 1919 I became restless and left for le Valais, there I applied Lipps' statistical method to a biometric study of the variability of land mollusks as a function of altitude! I needed to get back to concrete problems to avoid grave errors.

In the autumn of 1919 I took the train for Paris where I spent two years at the Sorbonne. I attended Dumas' course in pathological psychology (where I learned to interview mental patients at Sainte-Anne), and the courses of Piéron and Delacroix; I also studied logic and philosophy of science with Lalande and Brunschvicg. The latter exerted a great influence on me because of his historical-critical method and his references to psychology. But I still did not know what problem area of experimentation to choose. Then I had an extraordinary piece of luck. I was recommended to Dr. Simon who was then living in Rouen, but who had at his disposal Binet's laboratory at the grade school of the rue de la Grangeaux-Belles in Paris. This laboratory was not being used because Simon had no classes in Paris at this time. Dr. Simon received me in a very friendly manner and suggested that I should standardize Burt's reasoning tests on the Parisian children. I started the work without much enthusiasm, just to try anything. But soon my mood changed; there I was, my own master, with a whole school at my disposition—unhoped-for working conditions.

Now from the very first questionings I noticed that though Burt's tests certainly had their diagnostic merits, based on the number of successes and failures, it was much more interesting to try to find the reasons for the failures. Thus I engaged my subjects in conversations patterned after psychiatric questioning, with the aim of discovering something about the reasoning process underlying their right, but especially their wrong answers. I noticed with amazement that the simplest reasoning task involving the inclusion of a part in the whole or the coordination of relations or the "multiplication" of classes (finding the part common to two wholes), presented for normal children up to the age of eleven or twelve difficulties unsuspected by the adult.

Without Dr. Simon being quite aware of what I was doing, I continued for about two years to analyze the verbal reasoning of normal children by presenting them with various questions and exposing them to tasks involving simple concrete relations of cause and effect. Furthermore, I obtained permission to work with the abnormal children of the Salpétrière; here I undertook research on numbers, using the methods of direct manipulation as well as that of conversation. I have since resumed this work in cooperation with A. Szeminska.

At last I had found my field of research. First of all it became clear to me that the theory of the relations between the whole and the part can be studied experimentally through analysis of the psychological processes underlying logical operations. This marked the end of my "theoretical" period and the start of an inductive and experimental era in the psychological domain which I always had wanted to enter, but for which until then I had not found the suitable problems. Thus my observations that logic is not inborn, but develops little by little, appeared to be consistent with my ideas on the formation of the equilibrium toward which the evolution of mental structures tends; moreover, the possibility of directly studying the problem of logic was in accord with all my former philosophical interests. Finally my aim of discovering a sort of embryology of intelligence fit in with my biological training; from the start of my theoretical thinking I was certain that the problem of the relation between the organism and environment extended also into the realm of knowledge, appearing here as the problem of the relation between the acting or thinking subject and the objects of his experience. Now I had the chance of studying this problem in terms of psychogenetic development.

Once my first results had been achieved, I wrote three articles taking great care not to become biassed by theory. I analyzed the data, psychologically as well as logically, applying the principle of logical-psychological parallelism to my method of analysis: Psychology explains the facts in terms of causality, while logics when concerned with true reasoning describes the corresponding forms in terms of an ideal equilibrium[3] (I have since expressed this relation by saying that logic is the axiomatic whose corresponding experimental science is the psychology of thought).[4]

I sent my first article[5] to the *Journal de Psychologie* and had the pleasure not only of seeing it accepted, but also of noting that I. Meyerson who became my friend at this time had interests very similar to mine. He had me read Lévy-Bruhl and spurred me on by his encouragement and advice. He also accepted my second article.[6]

As for the third, I sent it to Ed. Claparède, whom I had met but once, and who published it in the *Archives de Psychologie*.[7] But in addition to accepting my article, he made a proposal which changed the course of my life. He offered me the job of "director of studies" at the Institut J. J. Rousseau of Geneva. Since he barely knew me, he asked me to

[3]Cf. Une forme verbale de la comparaison chez l'enfant, *Arch. de Psychol.*, 1921, *18*, 143–172.

[4]*Psychologie de l'intelligence* (1947), Chap. 1.

[5]Essai sur quelques aspects du developpement de la notion de partie chez l'enfant, *J. de Psychol.*, 1921, *38*, 449–480.

[6]Essai sur la multiplication logique et les débuts de la pensées formelles chez l'enfant, *J. de Psychol.*, 1922, *38*, 222–261.

[7]La pensée symbolique et la pensée chez l'enfant, *Arch. de Psychol.*, 1923, *38*, 273–304.

come to Geneva for a month's trial. This prospect enchanted me, as much because of Claparède's fame as for the wonderful research facilities which this position would afford; on the other hand, as yet I did not know how to start out on any research! I accepted in principle, and left Paris for Geneva. I noted immediately that Claparède and Bovet were ideal patrons who would let me work according to my desires. My work consisted simply of guiding the students and of associating them with the research that I was asked to undertake on my own, provided it was in child psychology. This was in 1921.

IV. 1921–1925

Being of a systematic turn of mind (with all the hazards that this implies) I made plans which I then considered final: I would devote two or three years more to the study of child thought, then return to the origins of mental life, that is, study the emergence of intelligence during the first two years. After having thus gained objectively and inductively a knowledge about the elementary structures of intelligence, I would be in the position to attack the problem of thought in general and to construct a psychological and biological epistemology. Above all, then, I would have to stay away from any non-psychological preoccupation and study empirically the development of thought for itself, wherever this might lead me.

According to this plan I organized my research at the Maison des Petits of the Institut J. J. Rousseau, starting with the more peripheral factors (social environment, language) but keeping in mind my goal of getting at the psychological mechanism of logical operations and of causal reasoning. In this connection I also resumed, working with the primary school pupils of Geneva, the type of investigation I had done in Paris.

The results of the research is contained in my first five books on child psychology.[8] I published them without taking sufficient precautions concerning the presentation of my conclusions, thinking they would be little read and would serve me mainly as documentation for a later synthesis to be addressed to a wider audience. (The studies were the product of a continuous collaborative effort in which all students of the Institute participated, among them Valentine Châtenay who became my wife and constant co-worker.) Contrary to my expectation, the books were read and discussed as if they were my last word on the

[8] *The language and thought of the child* (1924), *Judgment and reasoning in the child* (1924), *The child's conception of the world* (1926), *The child's conception of causality* (1927), *The moral judgment of the child* (1932).

subject, some adopting my point of view of a genesis of logic, others strongly opposing it (especially in circles influenced by empirical epistemology or Thomism). I was invited to many countries (France, Belgium, the Netherlands, England, Scotland, the United States, Spain, Poland, etc.) to present my ideas and discuss them before university faculties and other teachers. (However, I had no interest in pedagogy at that time as I had no children.) This unexpected acclaim left me somewhat uneasy, since I realized quite clearly that as yet I had not organized my ideas and had barely entered the preliminaries. But one cannot say to the critics, "Wait—you have not seen what is coming"— especially when one does not know it himself. Besides, when one is young he does not suspect that, for a long time, he will be judged by his first works, and that only very conscientious people will read the later ones.

Two essential shortcomings existed in these first studies. One I was not aware of before studying infant behavior; the other, however, I knew perfectly well.

The first of these shortcomings consisted in limiting my research to language and expressed thought. I well knew that thought proceeds from action, but I believed then that the language directly reflects acts and that to understand the logic of the child one had only to look for it in the domain of conversations or verbal interactions. It was only later, by studying the patterns of intelligent behavior of the first two years, that I learned that for a complete understanding of the genesis of intellectual operations, manipulation and experience with objects had first to be considered. Therefore, prior to study based on verbal conversations, an examination of the patterns of conduct had to be carried out. True enough, since one finds in the action of younger children all the characteristics he observes in the verbal behavior of older children, my first studies on verbal thought were not in vain; but my point of view would have been much more easily understood if I had found out then what I discovered only later: that, between the preoperative stage from two to seven years and the establishment of a formal logic occurring at the ages of eleven and twelve, there functions (between seven and eleven years of age) an organizational level of "concrete operations" which is essentially logical, though not yet formal-logical (for instance, the child of eight will be able to conclude $A < C$ if he has seen three objects under the form $B > A$ and $B < C$, but he will fail to perform the same operation on the purely verbal plane).

The second shortcoming stems from the first, but I did not quite understand the reasons then: I tried in vain to find characteristic structures-of-the-whole relative to logical operations themselves (again my theory of the part and the whole!); I did not succeed because I did not seek their source in concrete operations. So I satisfied my need for an explanation in terms of structures-of-the-whole by studying the social aspect of thought (which is a necessary aspect, I still believe, of the formation of logical operations as such). The ideal equilibrium (the reciprocal preservation of the whole and of the parts) pertains here to the cooperation between individuals who become autonomous by this very cooperation. Imperfect equilibrium characterized by the alteration of the parts in relation to the whole appears here as social constraint (or constraint of the younger by the older). Imperfect equilibrium characterized by the change of the whole as a function of the parts (and the lack of coordination of the parts) appears as unconscious egocentricity of the individual, that is, as the mental attitude of young children who do not yet know how to collaborate nor to coordinate their points of view. (Unfortunately, because of the vague definition of the term "egocentricity"—undoubtedly an ill-chosen term!—and because of the misunderstandings of the concept of mental attitude, this term has usually not been given its only clear and simple meaning.)

Though I failed at first to find the characteristic structures of logical operations which ought to correspond to the structures of social intercourse (at least I sensed at once the importance of the reversibility of thought).[9] I noticed that a certain degree of irreversibility of operations corresponded to the young child's difficulties in grasping intellectual and social reciprocity. But to put this hypothesis on solid ground I had first to study concrete operations.

During these years, I had discovered the existence of Gestalt psychology, so close to my notions concerning structures-of-the-whole. The contact with the work of Köhler and Wertheimer made a twofold impression on me. Firstly, I had the pleasure of concluding that my previous research was not sheer folly, since one could design on such a central hypothesis of the subordination of the parts to the organizing whole not only a consistent theory, but also a splendid series of experiments. In the second place, I felt that, though the Gestalt notion suited perfectly the inferior forms of equilibrium (those in which the part is altered by the whole or those in which, according to the very terms of the theory, there is no "additive composition"), it did not explain the kind of structure peculiar to logical or rational operations. For example, the sequence of whole numbers 1, 2, 3 ... etc. is a remarkable operative structure-of-the-whole, since numbers do not exist alone but are engendered by the very law of formation itself ($1 + 1 = 2$, $2 +$

[9] *Judgment and reasoning in the child* (1928), p. 169.

1 = 3, etc.). And yet this law of formation constitutes essentially an "additive composition." What I consider a superior form of equilibrium (the mutual preservation of the parts by the whole and of the whole by the parts) therefore escaped the Gestaltist explanation. From this I concluded that it was necessary to differentiate successive steps of equilibria and to integrate the search for types of structures with a more genetic approach.

V. 1925–1929

In 1925 my former teacher, A. Reymond, vacated his chair of philosophy at the University of Neuchâtel, and a part of its incumbency was given to me, though I was merely a doctor of sciences. (Since 1921, as *privat-dozent* in the Faculté des Sciences at Geneva, I also taught child psychology). My duties at this time were very heavy: They included (in the Faculté des Lettres) the teaching of psychology, of philosophy of science, of a philosophy seminar, and also, of two hours of sociology at the Institut des Sciences Sociales. In addition I continued to teach child psychology at the Institut J. J. Rousseau. Since one learns by teaching, I expected that this heavy schedule would at least bring me closer to epistemology. In fact, for four years I devoted the course on philosophy of science to the study of the development of ideas as it can be observed in the history of science as well as in child psychology. The opening lecture on this subject[10] has since been published.

During these years many other problems occupied me. In 1925 my first daughter was born and my second in 1927 (a boy followed them in 1931). With the help of my wife I spent considerable time in observing their reactions, and also subjected them to various experiments. The results of this new research has been published in three volumes that deal mainly with the genesis of intelligent conduct, ideas of objective constancy and causality, and with the beginnings of symbolic behavior (imitation and play).[11] It is not feasible to summarize these books; the first two have not been published in English, but the third (written much later) is now in the process of being translated.

The main benefit which I derived from these studies was that I learned in the most direct way how intellectual operations are prepared by sensory-motor action, even before the appearance of language. I concluded that in order to progress in my research on child logic I had to change my method, or rather to modify it by directing the

---

[10]Psychologie et critique de la connaissance, *Arch. de Psychol.*, 1925, *19*, 193–210.

[11]*La naissance de l'intelligence chez l'enfant* (1937); *La construction du réel chez l'enfant* (1937); *La formation du symbole chez l'enfant* (1945).

conversations toward objects which the child himself could manipulate.

In the course of experiments (undertaken in collaboration with my students at Neuchâtel and at Geneva), I had just discovered that children up to 12 years did not believe in the constancy of material quantity, e.g., of the weight and the volume of a lump of modeling clay that changed its shape by stretching or flattening. I had observed in my own children that between the sixth and tenth month they did not possess the notion of the permanence of an object disappearing from view (a watch hidden beneath a handkerchief, etc.). Between the beginnings of a notion of constancy or permanence of concrete objects and the final mastery of the concept of constancy of physical properties (weight, mass, etc.), there had to be successive stages in the development of ideas of constancy which could be studied in concrete situations rather than solely through language. Experiments on this problem I resumed again much later, after my return to Geneva, in collaboration with A. Szeminska and B. Inhelder.

Before leaving Neuchâtel, I concluded the research on mollusks by clearing up a question which had preoccupied me for many years, and which touched on the fundamental problem of the relation between hereditary structure and environment. Indeed, this last problem had always seemed to me to be central, not only for the genetic classification of organic forms (morphogeny), but also for psychological learning theory (maturation versus learning) and epistemology. Therefore it seemed worthwhile to me to utilize my zoological findings for studying, in however limited a way, that significant problem of morphogenesis. I have been aware of a variety of *Limnaea stagnalis* particularly abundant in the lake of Neuchâtel and remarkable for its adaptation to its environment. Its globular shape comes from the action of the waves which constantly force the animal to clamp itself to the stones, and thus cause an enlargement of the opening and shortening of the whorl during the period of growth. The problem was to determine whether these traits were hereditary. Observations on 80,000 individuals living in their natural environment and on many thousands grown in an aquarium led me to draw the following conclusions: (1) this variety exists only in large lakes and in those sections of the lakes where the water is roughest; (2) its traits are hereditary and survive in an aquarium after five or six generations; a pure species can be segregated which reproduces according to the Mendelian laws of cross-breeding. The variety is able to live outside the lakes; I deposited some of them in a pond where they are still thriving after twenty years. The hypothesis of chance mutation, independent of environmental stimulation, seems unlikely in this particular case, since nothing prevents this globular variety from living in any body of fresh water.[12] That experience has taught me not to explain the whole of mental life by maturation alone!

VI. 1929-1939

In 1929 I returned to the university of Geneva as Professor of History of Scientific Thought (in the Division of Science) and Assistant Director of the Institut J. J. Rousseau; in 1932 I became co-director, with Claparède and Bovet. Since 1936 I have also taught experimental psychology at the University of Lausanne one day a week. In addition, in 1929 I imprudently accepted the duties of director of the Bureau International Office de L'Education on the insistence of my friend Pedro Rossello, who had become its assistant director. For two reasons this international office, which now is working in close collaboration with UNESCO, interested me. In the first place it was able, through its intergovernmental organization, to contribute toward the improvement of pedagogical methods and toward the official adoption of techniques better adapted to the mentality of the child. Secondly, there was, so to speak, an element of sport in that venture. Rossello and I had succeeded in having accepted a new organization essentially on an intergovernmental basis. But on the day the statute was signed there were only three governments participating: the canton of Geneva (the Swiss government itself was represented but undecided), Poland and Ecuador. Moreover we were the subject of poorly repressed opposition (I am speaking to psychologists!) by the Institut de Coopération Intellectuelle. We had to act quickly and with diplomacy. A few years later between thirty-five and forty-five governments were represented at the annual conferences called by the Swiss government (today this organization is sponsored jointly by UNESCO and the International Office of Education). This job has certainly cost me a good deal of time I might possibly have spent more advantageously on research in child psychology, but at least I have learned from it quite a bit about adult psychology!

Added to these non-scientific labors were other administrative duties; I had in particular the task of reorganizing the Institut J. J. Rousseau which ceased to be private and became partially affiliated with the University.

[12]See Les races lacustres de la *Limnaea stagnalis*, L. Recherches sur les rapports de l'adaptation héréditaire avec le milieu, *Bull. biol. de la France et de la Belgique*, 1929, *18*, 424–455; and L'adaptation de la *Limnaea stagnalis* aux milieux lacustres de la Suisse romande, *Rev. suisse de Zool.*, 1929, *36*, Plates 3–6, 263–531.

The years from 1929 to 1939 cover a period filled with scientific endeavors. Three principal events stand out in retrospect.

First, the course in the History of Scientific Thought which I gave in the Faculté des Sciences at Geneva enabled me to promote more vigorously the project of a scientific epistemology founded on mental development, both autogenetic and phylogenetic. For ten successive years I studied intensely the emergence and history of the principal concepts of mathematics, physics and biology.

Secondly, I again resumed, on a larger scale than before, the research in child psychology at the Institut J. J. Rousseau. This work I carried out in collaboration with most able assistants, particularly A. Szeminska, and B. Inhelder, who now occupies the chair of child psychology. Thanks to them, a series of new experiments could be performed that dealt systematically with problems of action (manipulation of objects), whereby the conversation that was carried on with the subject exclusively involved the child's own manipulatory conduct. By this method I studied the development of numbers with A. Szeminska, that of the ideas of physical quantity with B. Inhelder; I also started studies of spatial, temporal and other relationships with E. Meyer. The most advanced of these studies were published around 1940,[13] at a time when psychologists no longer had the opportunity of enchanging their ideas across frontiers, or often, even of doing research. Thus these books were little read outside of French-speaking areas, though they were the first to develop fully a number of problems on which my first books hardly had touched.

In the third place, the study of concrete operations finally enabled me to discover the operative structures-of-the-whole that I had been seeking so long. I analyzed in children four to seven or eight years of age the relationship of part and whole (by asking them to add pearls to a group of predetermined magnitude), the sequences of asymmetrical relationships (by letting them construct series of prescribed order), and the correspondences, item by item (by making them build two or more corresponding rows), etc. These studies led me to understand why logical and mathematical operations cannot be formed independently: The child can grasp a certain operation only if he is capable, at the same time of correlating operations by modifying them in different, well-determined ways—for instance, by inverting them. These operations presuppose, as does any primary intelligent conduct, the possibility of making detours (which corresponds to what logicians call

---

[13]Piaget and A. Szeminska, *La genèse du nombre chez l'enfant* (1941); Piaget and B. Inhelder, *Le developpement des quantités chez l'enfant* (1941). *La genèse du nombre* will soon be translated into English.

"associativity") and returns ("reversibility"). Thus the operations always represent reversible structures which depend on a total system that, in itself, may be entirely additive. Certain of these more complex structures-of-the-whole have been studied in mathematics under the name of "groups" and "lattices;" operative systems of this sort are indeed of importance for the development of equilibria of thought. I sought for the most elementary operative structures-of-the-whole, and I finally found them in the mental processes underlying the formation of the idea of preservation or constancy. Simpler than the "groups" and the "lattices," such structures represent the most primitive parts of a part-whole organization: I have called them "groupings." For example, a classification (whereby the classes of the same rank order are always discrete and separate) is a grouping.

I presented my first paper on this subject, although I had not yet thoroughly mastered it, at the International Congress of Psychology at Paris in 1937. At that same time I was trying to determine the logical structure of groupings of classes and relationships of which I was able to isolate eight interdependent forms. I wrote an article in 1939 on this topic which P. Guillaume and I. Meyerson published in their "Collection Psychologique and Philosophique."[14]

VII. 1939–1950

The war spared Switzerland without our really knowing exactly why. However great his concern, an intellectual of my age (43 years), no longer subject to military service (I had been definitely released in 1916), could only cross his arms or go on with his work.

When the professor of sociology at the University of Geneva gave up his position in 1939, I was, without my knowledge, nominated to that post; I accepted the call. A few months later Claparède fell ill of a disease which was to be fatal; I took over his duties, and, in 1940 was given the chair of Experimental Psychology and named Director of the Psychology Laboratory (there I found an outstanding co-worker in Lambercier). I continued editing the *Archives de Psychologie*, first with Rey, and later with Rey and Lambercier. A Swiss Society of Psychology was founded shortly thereafter and I assumed the presidency of it for the first three years, collaborating with Morgenthaler in editing a new *Revue Suisse de Psychologie*. There was much work to be done.

From 1939 to 1945 I carried on two kinds of research. Firstly, on assuming the responsibility of the laboratory made famous by the names of Th. Flournoy and Ed. Claparède, I undertook, with the collaboration of Lambercier and various assistants, a long-range study on

---

[14] *Classes, relations et nombres. Essai sur la réversibilité de la pensée* (1942).

the development of perceptions in the child (until the age of adulthood). The aim of this study was to better understand the relationship of perception and intelligence, as well as to test the claims of the Gestalt theory (which had not convinced me with respect to the problem of intelligence). The first results of this research, which we are still continuing, have already appeared in the *Archives de Psychologie,*[15] they seem to us rather instructive for a theory of structure. Whereas logical structures deal only with one of the various aspects of the objects (class, number, size, weight, etc.), but as far as that aspect is concerned, are complete, the perceptual structures are for the most part incomplete because they are statistical or merely probable. It is because of this character of probability that the perceptual structures are not additive, but follow the Gestalt laws. These structures do not remain the same at all ages: They have a less active character in the child than in the adult, and are closer to the products of intelligence in the latter. These facts are of consequence in such matters as the degree of geometric-optical illusions as a function of age, the magnitude of perceptual constancy, etc.

Secondly, by utilizing a concrete experimental technique and analytical method of procedure, and with the assistance of my collaborators, I began research on the development of ideas of time, of movement, of velocity, as well as on behavior involving these concepts.[16]

In 1942 Piéron was kind enough to invite me to give a series of lectures at the Collége de France; that occasion enabled me to bring to our French colleagues—it was during the German occupation—testimony of the unshakable affection of their friends from outside. The main content of these lectures appeared shortly after the war in a small volume which is now available in English[17] as well as in German, Swedish, etc.

As soon as the war was over, social exchanges were resumed with renewed effort. The International Office of Education had never completely ceased to function during the years 1939 to 1945; it had served particularly as a clearing house for the sending of educational books to prisoners of war. When UNESCO was being organized, the Office of Education participated in the preparatory conferences and, later, in the annual general conferences which decided on general policies and the work to be carried out by the two institutions. After Switzerland joined UNESCO, I was named by my government President of the

[15]Recherches sur le développement des perceptions (Recherches I à XII), *Arch. de Psychol.,* 1942–1950.

[16]*Le développement de la notion de temps chez l'enfant. Les notions de mouvement et de vitesse chez l'enfant* (1946).

[17]Piaget, *The psychology of intelligence* (1950).

Swiss Commission of UNESCO and headed the Swiss delegation to the conferences at Bayreuth, Paris and Florence. UNESCO sent me as a representative to the meetings at Sèvre and Rio de Janeiro, and entrusted me with the editing of the pamphlet "The Right to Education"; I also held for several months the interim post of Assistant Director General in charge of the Department of Education. When M. Torrès-Bodet offered me this post for a longer period, he put me in a somewhat embarrassing position; actually, it did not take me long to decide between the international tasks and the appeal of my uncompleted research: I accepted the offered responsibility, but for only a short time. I recently accepted, however, membership on the Executive Council of UNESCO, having been elected to it by the general conference at Florence.

While on the subject of international relations, I might mention that in 1946 I had the pleasure of receiving an honorary degree from the Sorbonne; I had been given the same honor by Harvard in 1936 during the unforgettable ceremonies celebrating the tricentenary of that great university. In 1949 I received the honorary doctorate of the University of Brussels and, that same year, the title of Professor, *honoris causa,* of the University of Brazil at Rio de Janeiro. Nor, while writing in this vein, do I wish to fail to mention the pleasure I felt on becoming a member of the New York Academy of Sciences.

But postwar social activities did not cause me to neglect my work. On the contrary, I have gone on a little faster for fear I might not finish in time if the world situation should again become troubled. That explains my many publications. This increase in output, however, does not imply hasty improvisation; I have been working on every one of these publications for a long time.[18]

---

[18] I have often been asked where I found the time for so much writing in addition to my university work and international duties. I owe it first to the unusual quality of the men and, especially, of the women who have collaborated with me, and who have helped me much more than I can demonstrate here. After years spent in questioning children all by myself, with only small groups of students, latterly I have been helped by teams of assistants and colleagues who did not confine themselves to collecting facts, but took an increasingly active part in conducting this research. And then, too, I owe it to a particular bent of my character. Fundamentally I am a worrier whom only work can relieve. It is true I am sociable and like to teach or to take part in meetings of all kinds, but I feel a compelling need for solitude and contact with nature. After mornings spent with others, I begin each afternoon with a walk during which I quietly collect my thoughts and coordinate them, after which I return to the desk at my home in the country. As soon as vacation time comes, I withdraw to the mountains in the wild regions of the Valais and write for weeks on end on improvised tables and after pleasant walks. It is this dissociation between myself as a social being and as a "man of nature" (in whom Dionysian excitement ends in intellectual activity) which has enabled me to surmount a permanent fund of anxiety and transform it into a need for working.

First of all, with the help of B. Inhelder, I was able to carry out about thirty experiments on the development of spatial relations between the ages of 2 and 3, and 11 and 12,[19] a problem all the more complex because of the constant mutual interference of factors of perception and action. On the other hand, study of intellectual operations as the only reversible mental mechanisms (as opposed to perception, motor performance, etc., which are one-directional) led us to the investigation of the reactions of young children to an irreversible physical phenomena, such as that of mixture or change.[20] I also finished a study on the genesis of probability with B. Inhelder, which was extended to include the wider problem of induction.

Secondly, I was at last in a position to realize my old plan of writing a genetic epistemology.[21] At the death of Claparède I had given up the course in history of scientific thought to take over experimental psychology. Since I had enough experimental data on the psychological processes underlying logico-mathematical and physical operations, it seemed the right time to write the synthesis I had been dreaming about from the beginning of my studies. Instead of devoting five years to child psychology, as I had anticipated in 1921, I had spent about thirty on it; it was exciting work and I do not in the least regret it. But now was the time to conclude it, and that is what I attempted in this general study. It is basically an analysis of the mechanism of learning, not statically, but from the point of view of growth and development.

Lastly, the Colin publishers asked me to write a Traité de logique[22] with the twofold aim of presenting concisely the operative methods of logistics (or modern algebraic logic) and of developing my own ideas on this subject. I hesitated at first since I am not a logician by profession. But then I was tempted by the desire to construct a schematic outline of logistics which would correspond, on the one hand, to the steps in the formation of operations (concrete operations of class and relationship —formal operation, or the logic of propositions), and, on the other hand, to the kinds of structures the fundamental psychological importance of which I had previously discovered. Since then I have written a shorter work, not yet published, which deals with structures-of-the-whole (groups, "lattices" and groupings) which can be defined by means of three propositions (the logic of the 256 ternary operations).

[19]Piaget and Inhelder, *La représentation de l'espace chez l'enfant (1948)*; Piaget, Szeminska and Inhelder, *La géométrie spontanée chez l'enfant (1948)*.

[20]*La genèse de l'idée de hasard chez l'enfant* (1951).

[21]*Introduction à l'epistémologie génétique*. I. *La pensée mathématique*, II. *La pensée physique*, III. La pensée biologique, la pensée psychologique et la pensée sociologique (1949–50).

[22]*Traité de logique, esquisse d'une logistique operatoire* (1949).

CONCLUSION

My one idea, developed under various aspects in (alas!) twenty-two volumes, has been that intellectual operations proceed in terms of structures-of-the-whole. These structures denote the kinds of equilibrium toward which evolution in its entirety is striving; at once organic, psychological and social, their roots reach down as far as biological morphogenesis itself.

This idea is doubtless more widespread than is generally assumed; however, it had never been satisfactorily demonstrated. After more than thirty years' work on the higher aspects of that evolution, I should like one day to go back to the more primitive mechanisms; this is one reason why I am interested in infantile perceptions. The reversibility characteristic of the operations of logical intelligence is not acquired *en bloc,* but is prepared in the course of a series of successive stages: elementary rhythms, more and more complex regulations (semi-reversible structures) and, ultimately, reversible operative structures. Now this law of evolution, which dominates all mental development, corresponds no doubt to certain laws of structuration of the nervous system which it would be interesting to try to formulate in regard to qualitative mathematical structures (groups, lattices, etc.)[23] As to Gestalt-structures, they constitute only one particular type among possible structures, and these belong to regulations rather than to (reversible) operations. I hope to be able some day to demonstrate relationships between mental structures and stages of nervous development, and thus to arrive at that general theory of structures to which my earlier studies constitute merely an introduction.

VIII. 1950–1966[24]

The preceding pages show how I tried to sift out the motives and different stages of contributions which I have been able to make to our discipline. Doubtless this is what was expected of a "History of psychology through autobiographies," for such was the title of the American collection for which the directors Murchison and Boring wanted me to write this account. But since now I have the opportunity to complete it up until 1966, it may be useful to draw some conclusions from past experiences.

[23]Piaget, Le probleme neurologique de l'interiorisation des actions en operations reversibles, *Arch. de Psychol.,* 1946, *32,* 241–258.

[24]Jean Piaget, "Autobiographie" in "Jean Piaget et les sciences sociales," *Cahiers Vilfredo Pareto, 10,* 1966, translated by Sarah F. Campbell & Elizabeth Rütschi-Herrmann.

An autobiography is never objective and it is naturally up to the reader to straighten it out in the direction of impersonal truth. Nevertheless it is interesting in the sense that it furnishes some indication as to what an author wanted to do and how he understood himself. If we are dealing with an author who has been interpreted in very diverse ways, this may even be useful. In recent publications I have been considered in turn as "neo-associationist" (Berlyne), transcendentalist (Battro), neo-Gestaltist (Meili); I have been closely connected to the Marxist dialectic (Goldman, Nowinski), etc. or else as being dependent at certain points on Aristotle and St. Thomas Aquinas (Chauchard). All this is very honorable, but it might be desirable to have some more particulars about how they arrived at certain ideas. This is why, when one day my students at the Sorbonne asked me how I had arrived at the use of symbolic logic even though my education was in biology, I had to give an autobiographical answer.[25] Also, I found it necessary in a little book on the value of philosophy, having the philosophers in mind, to tell how I had broken away from them.[26] Including this one, this makes a little too many autobiographies, but, we must hope that they never contradict each other. But since I was asked to complete the one you have just read, I want to state how at the end of a life's work I have arrived at certain convictions in retrospective ways as well as in current ones.

First of all, the events that occurred during 1950 to 1966 can be reduced to four principal ones. In the first place, I had the good fortune and honor of being invited in 1952 to teach genetic psychology at the Sorbonne as regular professor, and I was able to keep this position (by commuting between Geneva and Paris) until 1963 when the increasing activity at the International Center of Genetic Epistemology in Geneva forced me to give up the Paris courses despite the pleasure and intellectual enrichment which I derived from them. Secondly, in 1956 I was able to create at the School of Sciences of the University of Geneva, with an eight-year grant from the Rockefeller Foundation and with support from the Swiss National Science Foundation, the above-mentioned Center of Epistemology. I have described elsewhere[27] in some detail this exciting adventure which consists in having specialists from very different disciplines (logicians, mathematicians, physicists, biologists, psychologists and linguists) cooperate in common research and continually combine theoretical inquiry with experimental analysis.

[25] *Bulletin de psychologie* (Paris), 1959–60, *13* n° 169, pp. 7–13.
[26] *Sagesse et illusions de la philosophie,* Paris (P. U. F.) 1965, Chap. I. [*Insights and Illusions of Philosophy.* New York: Thomas Y. Crowell Publishing Company, Inc., 1971.]
[27] *Ibid.,* pp. 43–55. [pp. 28–37].

Thirdly, because of the work of the Center and because of the intensive activity of our collaborators and assistants I had to cooperate on numerous publications. The list of them can be found in the meticulous and complete Bibliography compiled by B. Inhelder, and her teammates, on the occasion of an anniversary volume[28] . . . It is quite apparent that almost every work mentioned in the last period is the fruit of joint research, for the most part with B. Inhelder herself. Finally, during these years a certain number of administrative and international tasks (UNESCO, International Office of Education, etc.) have increased. I shall mention only one of the most pleasant ones: the foundation and development of the "International Union of Scientific Psychology" of which I had the honor to be the second president from 1954 to 1957, succeeding Piéron.

Having mentioned this, I shall return to the history of ideas, and I notice that according to what I wrote in 1950 (conclusion of VII), I announced the dual goal of orienting myself toward a more general theory of structures and toward closer ties between the biological and neurological fields. I was then quite young and the time has come to mention what in fact became of it and to draw a lesson from the experiences I've had since then. In reality, these expectations were not completely in vain, but I was able to achieve the goals only through more or less different channels from those I had in mind, and I want to reflect on them for a moment, at least on those concerning the structures. As far as the cognitive structures and the organic structures are concerned, it is evidently too early to think about the precise correspondences between the former and the nervous system, and we must wait until the beautiful hypotheses of McCulloch are broken down into numerous sectors. On the other hand, a joint study at the Center of Genetic Epistemology on the principal trends in contemporary biology has convinced me not only that there are parallel problems (in the fields of adaptation, development, etc.), which I had insisted on for a long time, but also there is a convergence of notions, or of certain ones, of the current biological solutions with what we find in the study of intelligence. I therefore wrote a work of ideas on this subject (*Biology and Knowledge*) which is intended to formulate or to specify the problems and which will be published before long by Gallimard in their collection edited by J. Rostand.

As to the questions of the general theory of structures, we have certainly made progress, in joint research which is becoming more and more necessary and on which I would like to insist in this autobiogra-

---

[28] *Psychologie et épistémologie génétiques, thèmes piagétians,* Dunod (Paris) 1966, pp. 7 à 38.

phy by substituting the plural for the singular, waiting for the term symbiography to be coined.

I. First we must point out, and still independently of this program about structures, the increasing importance I had to attribute to criticism, particularly in those favored cases where it finally led to true mutual control. Doubtless I was one of the most criticized psychologists of this century. My first publications on the language of the child, his representation of the world, and his notions of causality have (as mentioned in IV) sparked very lively controversies, but less with respect to what was truly lacking than to the notion itself of qualitative or structural transformations of thought during development. As these criticisms showed in general a more or less total lack of understanding of the problem itself, I did not pay much attention, since I was convinced that later research would furnish the necessary proofs and I did not publish any answers except to Susan and Nathan Isaacs. Since then I have had the satisfaction of solid support from N. Isaacs; to see M. Laurendeau and A. Pinard recently apply a lucid methodological criticism to my old critics using the new facts which they have accumulated;[29] to read a work of Jan Smedslund, where he developed in a new form my old hypotheses on egocentrism and intellectual decentration,[30] etc. It is therefore not about these old criticisms I want to speak.

But there have been during the past ten or fifteen years and while our results concerning preoperational reactions (nonconservation, etc.) and operational responses of the child were multiplying, a considerable number of researchers who took up our experiments, in general without continuing to contest the facts, but scrutinizing our interpretations. On such grounds criticism and discussion became particularly useful because before we can consider an hypothesis demonstrated of structures-of-the-whole and their construction progressing in a rhythm which cannot be indefinitely accelerated, it is important to try first of all other forms of explanation and to check their respective values closely.

Some of my decisive experiences have thus taught me the irreplaceable value of these mutual controls, but under the condition that they be instituted quite systematically and, which is much more difficult, in an atmosphere of sufficient reciprocity to achieve real progress. A few years ago, a remarkable French experimental psychologist, P. Fraisse, doubted somewhat a number of our results in the field of perception in general as well as about the notions of speed and time, in which he is

---

[29]M. Laurendeau et A. Pinard, *La pensée causale,* Paris (P. U. F.).

[30]J. Smedslund, *Les origines sociales de la décentration, La psychologie et Epistémologie génétiques,* Dunod 1966, pp. 159–168.

a specialist. Now these divergences which first sparked the controversy about the usual model were of such interest to us (without mentioning the solid friendship which developed from these contacts), we acquired two kinds of habits the value of which turned out to be decisive: to replicate each experiment of the other and to communicate our writings to each other before publishing in order to get a critical appraisal and in order to make sure that we were always understood by our partner. One can hardly imagine before using such a method how useful it is even as far as establishing facts is concerned, but even more so with respect to refining an interpretation other than one's own, because one misses distinguishing the nuances and implications, and by acquiring the knowledge of these one enriches his own perspective even when we do not come to complete agreement.

Somewhere else[31] I told of my similar experience with the logician E. W. Beth, before we were able, as with P. Fraisse, to write a book together. And that situation was much more serious, because I am not a logician by profession and it seemed impossible to reduce Beth's criticisms. But such positive results can come only from mutual control, if there is sufficiently continuous personal contact, but sometimes circumstances do not permit this.

This brings us back to the problem of structures, which is currently the most frequent subject of criticism and the most central one coming from authors in the USA and USSR whom I have little occasion to see with any continuity. The theses which are being opposed to mine are simple and to my mind much too simple: thought consists in constructing images of the object and in directing and organizing these images according to verbal signs, language itself constituting an adequate description of things; the activity of the subject would then be only the construction of faithful representations of reality and nothing would hinder therefore voluntarily accelerating this development through learning and social transmissions even to skipping stages or telescoping them into immediate acquisitions. From the pedagogical point of view, a perspective which allows teaching everything to the child at any stage is "optimistic," and I will have to be called a "pessimist" if I maintain that in order to assimilate what we teach him, the child needs structures which he builds through his own activity.

If I could have a continuous contact with such authors, for example J. Bruner, who believes he has renewed the explanation of conservation with his theory of semiotic images and instruments, I would never cease to be astounded at the fact that the representatives of large

---

[31] *Sagesse et illusions de la philosophie,* p. 50. [*Insights and Illusions of Philosophy,* pp. 33–34.]

countries who intend to transform the world have no ambition other than to characterize the subject's activities as constructing images according to an adequate language. Before being convinced otherwise, I believed that action consists in changing reality and not in imitating it, and I would not have imagined that sputniks could be invented or trips to the moon be planned if one had been satisfied with copying observable—or already observed—facts. That a school-teacher of the old school who never invented anything may call optimistic the ideal consisting in teaching students as much and as early as possible I can understand, but that creative minds would bother with an idea such as attributing to each child a capacity for invention and reinvention (and with the time that any effective construction presupposes) is beyond my comprehension. In short, to take seriously operations and operational structures means to believe that the subject is able to transform reality, whereas a supposed primacy of images and language leads to a model of intelligence and of man that is fundamentally conservative. Is intelligence basically invention or representation? Such is the problem: now we cannot explain invention simply as a game of representations, while these already correspond to an important part of active structuration.

II. Do these theses go beyond the limits of psychology? Yes, indeed, with respect to their meaning but certainly not with respect to their verification. One of the apparent motives of the authors who do not trust the ideas of structures and operations is their fear of going outside psychology and calling upon logical and epistemological considerations. The decisive experience which I had during this last decade and especially in our Center of Genetic Epistemology has convinced me, on the contrary, of the necessity for interdisciplinary research and of its fruitfulness for the solution of specifically and authentically psychological problems. All that I have been able to achieve during the last ten years was indeed conceived and worked out in collaboration with B. Inhelder, just as before, but also with psychologists, logicians, mathematicians, physicists, biologists and cyberneticians at our Center. Without their constant support the problem of structures would not have advanced a single step. On the contrary, by relating the formal geneologies of structures with psychogenetic relationships in their concrete realizations and with cybernetic models of feedback control and their biological realizations, we begin to understand how operational structures form a bridge between the organization of life and logico-mathematical realities. But, I repeat, the increasing coherence and similarity of these hypotheses are the result of our continuous collaboration and not the lonely work of an individual scientist.

However, the question which comes up time and again during these years is that of the legitimacy of these interdisciplinary exchanges, because the same writers whom I mentioned before in regard to their critical attitude, oppose any intrusion of logic or epistemology into psychology and often accuse me of leaving its boundaries by talking of structures and operations. This is indeed so with J. Bruner in his last book[32] and this critical position is the more curious because Bruner is one of the first to talk to us about "strategies" and who tried to use game or decision theory in the solution of problems of intelligence (stating in this connection that "operation as Piaget calls it" is a strategy) and while neglecting the other operations of our "groupings" he keeps mentioning identity which is an operation like any other!

Let's see where this rejection of the interdisciplinary leads us, since this is a vital question for the future of our work ... The first fact we have to state is that in the long run no author will be able to stay within the boundaries of psychology without ever going outside of it. For example, J. Bruner's doctrine opposing my structural hypotheses calls for the intervention of at least three factors: image, language and communication between individuals (he also mentions action without knowing quite what to do with it, which is interesting, because that is where operations start). As far as the image is concerned we first have to establish its relation with perception or with interiorized imitation and the motor outline, which is a subject for the neurologists. This presupposes a collaboration between psychology and neurology, which is expected by practically everybody (or almost) and which has to be called interdisciplinary. Social communication also contains a sociological dimension, and collaboration between psychology and sociology is equally acceptable, at least in principle. But dealing with language has quite different implications: ... N. Chomsky[33] teaches that the functioning of language brings about a "generative grammar" whose use calls for constant activity of the subject and shows the intervention of structures which are closely related to logical structures; also Chomsky does not hesitate to consider these structures as preformed in the sense of being innate, and he goes even further than we do when we speak only of progressive equilibration and becoming "necessary," but not of being innate in the proper sense of the word.... And fourth, no psychologist ever went so far as to deny the presence in human intelligence and the child's progressive construction of that fundamental and admirably rich sequence of "natural" or whole numbers. Why should we in

[32]J. S. Bruner et al, *Studies in Cognitive Growth*. J. Wiley, 1966. Furthermore, let me hasten to thank my friend Bruner for dedicating this work to me.

[33]*Editor's note*. At Massachusetts Institute of Technology.

such a case be afraid of logical operations and structures, since numbers emanate directly from them? I personally fear that this might be another sign of the almost incurable conservatism of certain psychologists. They do not distrust numbers or mathematics because they have heard about them every day for 25 centuries, whereas they show protective repressions as soon as terms from modern logic or epistemology are mentioned.

This leads me to the central problem of our positions: it is not possible to have psychology of cognitive functions without resorting to logical models, especially without continuous epistemological analysis. On these two points criticisms addressed to me seemed to be the most systematic (either explicit or implied) because the traditional psychologist is ready to collaborate with the neurologist, sociologist, economist, linguist . . . whereas logic and epistemology belong to "philosophy" and do not concern him in the least. To this I can give two complementary answers (let me come back to philosophy in III), one starting from mathematical structures, the other from biology.

Nobody would deny that intelligence, including the child's, can master the entire set which we call "natural" numbers, just because it is reached from a prescientific level. How do they do it? It is useless to answer that numbers are present in the language and transmitted socially, because we would have to find out how the numbers were ever constructed in "primitive" societies and how each generation of children can understand them. The data we could collect on this point have been found in such diverse surroundings and as far away as Aden and Hong Kong, but we still have the problem of interpretation. The question we then ask our adversaries is simply: can we say anything of value about numbers without having some idea about what number consists of? If we suppose that cardinal number is a quality of objects, as claimed by Kotarbinsky ("my fingers are five," he once said to me at the Academy of Sciences of Poland) and once even Gonseth (by comparing it to color or transparency of a solid), is it acquired in the same way as if it is the result of placing into correspondence between classes (Frege, Whitehead, Russell, etc.) or as I maintain of a synthesis of inclusive nesting and of seriation? Is the order inherent in ordinal number a quality of things or does it come from the very action of putting into order (cf. the works of the behaviorist Berlyne on the learning order which comes around to the hypothesis of necessity for a "counter")? To deal with the acquisition of number while refusing to pose these problems seems to me to be a sign of the same imprudence as invoking the role of language while forgetting Chomsky's generative grammar, because ignoring the possible epistemological solutions does not mean being protected against all epistemology, but simply choosing the one of common sense, with its naive realism, as well as forgetting the linguistics of the linguist, means to retain nevertheless opinions which are current or from the "common sense" of pedagogy.

In other words, if we limit ourselves to a static psychology of the adult only or to such and such a phase of evolution it is easy to establish boundaries between psychology and epistemology. But as soon as we try, which has been my constant aim, to explain behavior and mental mechanisms by their development, and above all by their very formation, we find ourselves by this mere fact constantly and absolutely forced to decide what in this formation depends upon the object, what on the activities of the subject, or what on the interaction between them and in what form. Now here we are, whether we like it or not, faced with epistemological problems and if we do not want to work in the dark or remain dependent on naive epistemology, the first responsibility of genetic psychologists is to keep informed of epistemological solutions and to check them against the data they collect.

My second answer has always been, but even more so during these last years, that such a point of view is demanded of us by biology itself, because the central biological problem of the relations between the organism and the environment includes and dominates the relation between intelligence and reality, i.e., between the subject and the object. One of the founders of contemporary ethology, K. Lorenz, has also frequently pointed out in recent articles that it is impossible to have animal psychology without dealing with the epistemological problem. If this is true of Lorenz's geese and ducks, which lead him to Kantianism, I would also like to be listened to in the name of human children and adolescents who are leading me to a genetic and interactionist structuralism. My recent work on *Biology and Knowledge* presents abundant reasons for that.

III. But that does not mean at all that psychology should be reintegrated into philosophy from which it separated at one time, because interdisciplinary research presupposes common methods of experimental verification or of formal deduction and there is nothing common between scientific verification and speculation or pure philosophical "reflection." Last year I wrote a little book on *Insights and Illusions of Philosophy* wherein I try to show that the only "knowledge" is that which can be verified, i.e., scientific knowledge (which does not mean that I favor positivism which limits the latter instead of leaving it open indefinitely); and metaphysics reaches only "wisdom," i.e., a rational belief but containing part of the decisions or evaluation which surpasses knowing. There can be several kinds of wisdom, this little work concludes, whereas there is only one "truth."

This book will be translated into different languages[34] and it is too early yet to judge the acceptance of these theses. But in the French-speaking countries where I expected it to create a scandal, I was surprised by a number of favorable reactions or objectively differentiated ones. The best philosopher of French-speaking Switzerland today, J.-Cl. Piguet, agreed with me in the past and does now and denies me only to anticipate the future of metaphysics which could in the meantime discover its own decisive method. Since this is what we have been expecting for 25 centuries I am ready to renew the lease. In France, the Rationalist Union organized a public debate at the Sorbonne where I came to grips with the excellent philosopher P. Ricoeur and with a friend of J.-P. Sartre, F. Jeanson. Starting from the minimal idea of "wisdom" Ricoeur defended especially the idea that it presupposes "reason," which seems to me to be entirely acceptable because a decision can still come from reason without therefore leading to "truths." Whereas Jeanson gave me the great pleasure when he wanted to defend Sartre of reproaching me for centering my criticism on his first works of philosophical psychology, now outdated, and, as he mentioned, he does not believe in them any more. P. Fraisse took advantage of this and asked him to say so and he noted with pleasure how little the philosophers of today believed in this philosophical psychology which was one of the main objects of my attacks (and, may I add that some have the courage to want to revive it in the French-speaking part of Switzerland while it is losing its foothold more and more in France). Ricoeur, recognizing Sartre's errors answered by limiting the problem of philosophical psychology to that of "meaning"; but either we are dealing with cognitive meaning and we remain in the scientific domain, or we deal with human "meaning" in general and then it is a matter of values and of simple "wisdom."

IV. I tried to show (in II) the considerable role that teamwork and interdisciplinary work played for me during these past years. I must say the same for our strictly psychological research, but as far as it is divided up according to chapters or fields which are usually separated and originate from different specialities or specialists: intelligence, perception, imagery, memory, learning, etc. Two remarks have to be made in this respect.

In most institutes research is multiple but each scientist specializes and keeps his limited field for years. Private conversations however or periodic meetings with exposés by all of them keep the group of specialists informed of what is being done, but everyone follows his own line

[34]*Editor's note.* Wolfe Mays, translator for the English Edition.

more or less independently. The organization of research which we tried to achieve consists to the contrary in choosing a common task that will occupy those who do the research, the head investigators, and the assistants for a few years time. These researchers are gathered once a week by B. Inhelder and myself in order to polish up the techniques and the results. Temporary formulation which I usually take on is criticized by everyone for the benefit of new controls and new projects. This is done again and again until we have the feeling that we are no longer finding anything new. This organization was partially accomplished for a long time with respect to the development of thought, but at the time of our research on perception, there were still two separate working groups instead of one and they did not have enough contact. Since then we have gotten united.

After this we had the problem of assigning to this closely knit team sufficiently large goals, i.e., to find study projects which go beyond the limits of only intellectual operations. The mental image is naturally located between perception and intelligence, and we devoted a few years to that question, starting with suggestions from all of us and pursuing new research in order to control the previous one, as well as pursuing incidental ideas as they came up. One of the problems was the relations between images and operations, but this was by far not the only one in the beginning, and if we kept coming back to it, it was because the evolution of imaged representations in the child shows clearly that the image in itself is not sufficient and does not progress (from the static to the dynamic and to images of transformation, or from simple reproduction to anticipation) unless it is subordinated to operations. A large collective volume[35] is the result of these efforts.

Research on learning, directed by B. Inhelder, M. Bovet and H. Sinclair, in which I had no part, originated in the work of the Center of Epistemology on the learning of logical structures and especially studies by B. Inhelder in some cases which were followed longitudinally. One of the essential problems was to find out how a child passes from one operational stage to the next and the difficult analysis of the factors of acquisition was advanced in such a way that it shows, then and now, clearly the insufficiency of only the ones Bruner retains. The psycholinguistic studies of H. Sinclair[36] indicate in themselves alone how much the development of language seems to depend on that of operations, rather than the opposite.

[35]Piaget, Inhelder, et. al, L'image mentale chez l'enfant. Paris (P. U. F.), 1966. [Mental Imagery in the Child, translated by P. A. Chilton. New York: Basic Books, 1971.]

[36]H. Sinclair de Zwart, Acquisition du language et developpement de la pensée, Dunod (in press).

The study of images had to lead us sooner or later to that of memory images and here we thought we would completely leave the field of operations when we first analyzed the memories with the corresponding operational structure. Now all during this research, which occupied us for a long time, we kept falling back into a systematic dependency of memory upon the operational schemes. To mention only one example, the sight of a collection of ten sticks, arranged in order, without any manipulation by the child, after a week is recalled as pairs, trios, etc., which expresses the manner in which the model was assimilated to the subject's operational level and not his simple perception; furthermore, after six months seventy-five per cent of these remembrances improved (without any further presentation) as a function of the progression of the scheme as if intelligence alone led to a reconstruction of the initial inputs. These results will be published.

In other words, a team dealing with usually separate chapters has indeed led us to renew somewhat our field of studies, which was very restricted in the beginning, but afterwards especially led us to see the fundamental unity of these fields which are often treated separately from each other. The interdisciplinary methods are fruitful right into the core of the relations which could be called inter-sub-disciplinary, at the heart of psychology itself.

Our projects for the future are many and varied. I shall mention only one which already achieved a sort of renewal in the field of cognitive operations. While studying the development of logico-mathematical operations, we insisted particularly on the spontaneous actions of the subject, because we were dealing with the results of his actions and his thought. But ever since an old and outdated work of ours we had somewhat neglected causality, starting with action itself in its causal effects and not in its internal logic. Now, causality is an operation attributed to objects and not simply applied to them. To take up the study of causality systematically again, we start with the analysis of cognitive development by considering the point of view of the object and no longer of the subject. This is an immense field which might hold many surprises. But thinking in terms of a life's work it ought to be better to change one's perspectives than be condemned to repeating oneself forever.

NAME INDEX

SUBJECT INDEX